Filmguide to

INDIANA UNIVERSITY PRESS FILMGUIDE SERIES
Harry Geduld and Ronald Gottesman,
General Editors

Filmguide to

Psycho

JAMES NAREMORE

INDIANA UNIVERSITY PRESS
Bloomington London

Published in Canada by Fitzhenry & Whiteside Limited, Don Mills, Ontario
Library of Congress catalog card number: 72-88636
ISBN: 0-253-39307-8 cl.   0-253-39308-6 pa.
Manufactured in the United States of America

2 3 4 5 6   80 79 78 77 76

For Jay, who likes horror movies

I would like to thank Harry Geduld and Ron Gottesman for giving me this opportunity. My thanks also to Murray Sperber and Charles Eckert, who spent hours talking with me about *Psycho*.

J.N.

contents

Filmguide to

Psycho

credits

PSYCHO

Paramount Pictures,1960   *Producer:* Alfred Hitchcock

Direction	Alfred Hitchcock
Screenplay	Joseph Stephano, from the novel by Robert Bloch
Photography	John L. Russell, A.S.C.
Special Effects	Clarence Champagne
Art Direction	Joseph Hurley, Robert Clatworthy
Sets	George Milo
Music	Bernard Herrmann
Sound Engineering	Waldon Watson, William Russell
Title Design	Saul Bass
Editing	George Tomasini
Assistant Director	Hilton Green
Costumes	Helen Colvig
Time	109 minutes

Filmed in Hollywood, partly on the lots of the old Universal Studios. Interiors filmed at Revue Studios. Locations: Route 99 of the Fresno–Bakersfield Highway; the San Fernando Valley; a Hollywood thoroughfare.

New York Premiere: June 16, 1960, DeMille and Baronet Theatres.

3

CAST

Norman Bates	Anthony Perkins
Marion Crane	Janet Leigh
Lila Crane	Vera Miles
Sam Loomis	John Gavin
Milton Arbogast	Martin Balsam
Sheriff Chambers	John McIntire
Mrs. Chambers	Laureen Tuttle
Carolyn	Pat Hitchcock
Cassady	Frank Albertson
Dr. Richmond	Simon Oakland
George Lowrey	Vaughn Taylor
Car Salesman	John Anderson
Policeman	Mort Mills
Officials	Sam Flint, Francis DeSales; George Eldredge
A man in a cowboy hat	Alfred Hitchcock

outline

A cautionary note: *Psycho* was designed to shock its audience, and on the first viewing it ought to be approached in relative innocence. If you have never seen the film, you should read no further. The following plot summary is intended only to refresh the memories of initiates; I have tried to keep it brief, saving the details for a scene by scene analysis.

Psycho opens in Phoenix, Arizona. It is Friday, December eleventh, two forty-three p.m., and we discover a half-dressed man and woman in a dingy hotel room. The man is Sam Loomis, a hardware store owner from Fairvale, California; the woman is Marion Crane, a real-estate secretary on her lunch hour. Marion, who looks to be in her thirties, is living in quiet desperation, alone except for her younger sister. She has been stealing moments like these for some time, but she is growing weary, beginning to long for marriage and respectability. Sam, on the other hand, has been married once before, and between his alimony payments and the debts he has inherited from his father, all of his money is being used up. He tells Marion that he cannot support her.

Though she has a headache, Marion returns to work, where she is surrounded with people who have money or marriage. Her boss brings a wealthy, drunken client back from lunch, and the client takes forty thousand dollars from his wallet, boasting that he is going to buy a happy home for his daughter. Marion's boss nervously asks her to put the cash in a safety deposit box over the weekend until the deal can be closed properly. Pleading her headache, Marion leaves early; when we next see her she is in her bedroom, preparing to steal the money and run away to Fairvale. She packs her bags and starts to drive away, but before she escapes Phoenix her boss notices her at a city stoplight. Anxiously, she drives on throughout the afternoon and evening, never pausing, until she is so fatigued that she has to pull over to the side of the road for sleep.

On the following morning she is wakened by a highway policeman, who becomes suspicious of her behavior. He lets her go and she drives off, entering a small town where she uses part of the stolen money to exchange cars. Again her stratagem fails, because the curious policeman has followed her and is watching as she leaves with the new car. Still she goes on, becoming more and more frightened: She imagines the voices of her pursuers, and as night falls she loses her way in a rainstorm. When the rain slackens, she pulls up at the Bates Motel, a forgotten, unfrequented place off the main road, situated just in front of an eerie Gothic mansion.

The motel is run by a friendly but somewhat strange young man named Norman Bates, who lives with his mother in the old house. Norman explains to Marion that she is only a few miles from Fairvale, and after she registers with a false name he invites her up to his place for sandwiches. Marion accepts the offer, but while she is in her room unpacking she overhears the sounds of an argument coming from the Bates' home. Norman returns, apologizing for his mother, and suggests that Marion might like to have her meal in the "parlor" behind the motel office. There, surrounded by stuffed birds of prey, Norman explains to Marion that his mother is mentally ill; many years ago, after she became a widow, her lover died under peculiar circumstances, and ever since Norman has sacrificed his life to care for her. He refuses to commit her to an asylum, he says, because he is angered by the dispassionate cruelty of such places. As Norman talks about madness and the "traps" people find themselves living in, Marion begins to take a more rational view of her own situation. She returns to her room, thanking Norman for his help, having decided to return the stolen money before its loss can be discovered.

When Marion has gone, we watch Norman study the false name on the motel registry. He removes a painting from a wall in the parlor, spying on his guest as she takes off her clothes. Soon he replaces the picture and leaves, walking morosely back to the old house. A few moments later, while Marion is taking a shower, the shadowy figure of an old woman enters the motel bathroom and brutally stabs her to death.

Discovering what his "mother" has done, Norman rushes back to the motel, recoiling in horror at the scene in the bathroom. He takes a grip on himself and proceeds to hide the crime: He cleans away the bloodstains, wrapping Marion's body in a shower curtain and stuffing it into the trunk of her car. Driving to a nearby swamp, he sends all the evidence (including the stolen money, which he does not know about) to the bottom of a muddy pond.

A week passes. Lila Crane, Marion's sister, has become alarmed, and the real-estate office has hired a private detective to try to recover the forty thousand dollars. Lila and detective Arbogast arrive in rapid succession at Sam Loomis' hardware store in Fairvale, only to find that Sam knows nothing of what has happened. Arbogast searches in hotels and rooming houses all around town, ultimately coming upon the Bates Motel, where Norman arouses his suspicions. After calling Lila to inform her of what he has found, Arbogast returns secretly to the motel at night to question Mrs. Bates. He enters the old house without knocking, but as he is going upstairs to investigate, a maniacal woman rushes upon him with a knife.

When they hear nothing from Arbogast, Sam and Lila try to investigate on their own. First Sam goes to the motel, finding it deserted, and then he and Lila take the matter to the local sheriff. They awaken Sheriff Chambers and his wife in the middle of the night, explaining their fears, but the sheriff will not be persuaded. He has known the hermit-like Norman Bates for some time and he believes that Arbogast was lying. Mrs. Bates, he says, has been dead for ten years.

Sam and Lila talk the sheriff into making a brief phone call to Norman, who claims that he knows nothing about Arbogast. This call alarms Norman, and he decides to put "Mother" in the fruit cellar, where she will be removed from prying eyes. We watch him carry a limp but talkative and protesting body down to the lower depths of the old house. On the next morning, a Sunday, Sam and Lila meet the sheriff outside of Fairvale Church, trying once more to persuade him to investigate. When the sheriff again refuses, they drive out to the Bates Motel on their own. They register as man and wife, and although Norman sees through their ruse, he gives them a room. After Norman is out of sight, they begin a search, uncovering in Cabin One a scrap of paper which indicates that Marion has been there. While Sam goes to the motel office to keep Norman busy, Lila steals up to the house, hoping to talk with Mrs. Bates. There she discovers the strange bedrooms of Norman and his mother. Meanwhile Sam has begun to threaten Norman, accusing him of killing Marion for the forty thousand dollars; as it dawns on Norman that Lila is in his house, he bashes Sam on the head and rushes out in panic. But Lila hears Norman returning, and she goes down to the fruit cellar to hide.

In the cellar, Lila encounters Mrs. Bates, who is nothing more than a hideously mummified body. She screams and Norman dances in, dressed like his mother, brandishing a knife. Sam has recovered, however, and enters the cellar just in time to subdue the maniac before he can murder again.

Later, at the Fairvale courthouse, a psychiatrist explains what has happened. Norman Bates had been raised by his widowed mother, and was obsessively jealous. When Mrs. Bates took a lover, Norman murdered them both, preserving his mother's body with taxidermy, then impersonating her in order to keep her alive in his own mind. A schizophrenic, Norman had probably killed other women before Marion Crane arrived at the motel. Now, we are told, the "mother" half of his personality has taken over entirely. In the last scene, we see what is left of Norman, a huddled figure in a barred cell, speaking with its mother's voice, pleading innocence and staring with sinister eyes back at the audience. The image of a skull is gradually superimposed over the madman's face; as the scene dissolves, Marion Crane's auto is shown being hauled up out of its swampy grave.

the director: Alfred Hitchcock and the aesthetics of repression

Psycho is enhanced by the performances of Janet Leigh and Tony Perkins, by the photography of John Russell, and by the music of Bernard Herrmann. But before anything else, it is an expression of Alfred Hitchcock's personality and it owes its greatness to him. We are dealing here with a director's movie, and it is logical to begin with a few remarks about Hitchcock's career.

First, a brief rehearsal of some relatively well-known facts. Hitchcock was born in London in 1899, and was educated by the Jesuits at St. Ignatius College. He briefly studied engineering and art, but his fascination with the movies led him to take a job as illustrator of title cards for the English branch of the Famous Players Studio. When Famous Players dissolved, he worked with other companies as writer, assistant director, and art director, living briefly in Berlin, where he was employed by UFA, the wealthy German studio which had produced many of the expressionist masterpieces, including the early work of Lang and Murnau. He directed his first complete film in 1925, a romantic melodrama called *The Pleasure Garden*; but the first true "Hitchcock movie" was *The Lodger* (1926), a Jack-the-Ripper murder story based on the Belloc-Lowndes novel. In 1928, he made the first British all-talking picture, *Blackmail,* a brilliant work which is remembered in the histories chiefly for its experimentation with expressive sound. During the thirties, he gained international success with a series of hits released by Gaumont British and Gainsborough Pictures: *The Man Who Knew Too Much, The Thirty-Nine Steps, The Secret Agent, Sabotage, Young and Innocent,* and *The Lady Vanishes.* As a result of these classic and immensely popular thrillers, Hitchcock was wooed by Hollywood, and came to America in 1939 under contract with David Selznick. His American debut was *Rebecca* (1940), which won the Academy Award as best picture of the year. In the forties, two of his films were given wide-spread critical praise—*Shadow of a Doubt* (1943) and *Notorious* (1946) —but the next major period of his work did not begin until 1951. Over the following twelve years, in rapid succession, he produced and directed *Strangers on a Train, I Confess, Rear Window, To Catch a Thief, The Trouble with Harry, The Man Who Knew Too Much* (a remake), *The Wrong Man, Vertigo, North by Northwest, Psycho,* and *The Birds.* Also during the fifties, his successful American television show, *Alfred Hitchcock Presents,* gave him a fame and popularity virtually unprecedented for a movie director. His latest film, as of this writing, is *Frenzy* (1972), in which he returns to his native London and to the ladykiller themes of his earliest work.

Until fairly recently, critics argued heatedly over the value of Hitchcock's American films. The argument persists, but it has grown trivial and more than a little snobbish. At one time his American work was grossly underrated, but today it is recognized by all but a few respectable dissenters (and what artist has not had them?) as the highest achievement of an important creative talent. If anything, it is Hitchcock's British masterpieces that now suffer neglect, though it is doubtful that anyone will make a persuasive case that they are superior to his best American films. Whatever the course of his future, the director of *Psycho* has earned himself a secure place in most critical pantheons.

Hitchcock has been stereotyped as the "Master of Suspense," a label that seems superficial and condescending. If suspense were his only virtue, why would we enjoy watching his best pictures again and again? Nevertheless, it should be clear that his artistic preoccupations are naturally suited to, and partly developed by, his work as a director of thrillers. In fact his chief literary influence, insofar as he can be said to have one, is the English novelist John Buchan, the author of the original *Thirty-Nine Steps* and the inspiration for *The Man Who Knew Too Much*. In Buchan's work we can detect a theme which becomes increasingly manifest in Hitchcock and in virtually every subsequent practitioner of the suspense story: In 1913, Buchan wrote about an ordinary fellow named Lethen, who found himself being pursued "like a thief" down a London thoroughfare on a perfectly pleasant June afternoon. "I suddenly realized," this character remarks, "how thin was the protection of civilization!" Many years later Graham Greene was to comment on the importance that particular line had for his own work; Buchan, Greene said, was "the first to realize the enormous dramatic value of adventure in familiar surroundings happening to unadventurous men."

Obviously, the same idea was attractive to Hitchcock, who tells us in his interview with François Truffaut that Buchan was a "strong influence." "What I find most appealing," Hitchcock says, "is his understatement of highly dramatic ideas." By contemporary standards, Buchan may seem anything but understated, but Hitchcock is pointing to the essentially "unadventurous" quality of the surroundings. He has said that he dislikes the ordinary, yet one of the most important attributes of his work is his ability to amuse, excite, and terrify us by evoking the sinister out of the commonplace; generally speaking, his killers are not scarfaced monsters who stand under city streetlights; they are more likely to be your Uncle Charlie or that nice Norman Bates. Even in *Psycho,* which uses some of the most outlandish machinery from traditional horror movies, the real menace arrives not in the old dark house, but in a completely sanitary motel bathroom. The greatest moments in Hitchcock's films have had settings which are so placid, so ridiculously incongruous, that they are sometimes like grand overstatements of his leading idea: a killer's face unmoving in the audience at a tennis match; a murderous airplane swooping down to attack an ad executive stranded on a midwestern prairie in broad daylight. These scenes depict nighttime fantasies obtruding on a daytime existence—they are sudden ruptures of the rational, civilized order that we like to think is secure. Thus, when that kindly, sympathetic, entirely admirable English gentleman in *The Thirty-Nine Steps* holds up a hand to show that the little finger is missing, we feel an absurdity, a sensation of vertigo. When his sweet, attractive wife comes in, glances at the revolver he is holding and casually announces something about the guests, the whole world becomes topsy-turvy. Suddenly, and in an essentially witty manner, the center cannot hold; mere anarchy is loosed upon the world; the ceremony of innocence is drowned.

It was Freud, of course, who observed the relationship between wit and the unconscious, arguing that jokes are therapeutic indulgences of our darker, anarchic instincts. In Freud's view, we need comedy in order to maintain our sanity, in order to release the frustrations caused by a repressive, albeit necessary social order. Whatever the merits of this theory, the satire and absurdist wit in Hitchcock's films seem to derive from a roughly similar view of life; he is not a straight-forward explicator of Freud's ideas (even if on occasion he has tried to be), yet he is clearly a great humorist of anxiety. Moreover, virtually every strong emotional effect in his work, whether comic or not, is nurtured by repressive counterforces. He wants to show us fear and disorder being restrained by and then ultimately breaking through a complacent, usually middleclass surface. Especially in his early work in Britain, he tried to create films that would be faithful to ordinary English life. He complained, for example, that the "extreme effects" of setting were "much the easiest to register," and he tried, in films like *Blackmail* and *Sabotage,* to achieve "a real lower-middle class atmosphere." Such an atmosphere was not valuable to Hitchcock purely for the sake of social realism; he wanted it because he felt the inherent dramatic value of disrupting the quiet, mundane surroundings.

Consider, for example, his treatment of sexuality, where we can see the process at work most clearly. The women in his films are nearly all "defrocked nuns," to use James Cavill's phrase—in fact, one of the major plot turns of *The Lady Vanishes* comes when the protagonists discover a nun wearing high heels. Hitchcock's ladies are cool, serene blondes who are typically well buttoned-up; but underneath their placid exteriors they are burning with passion. In this regard, it is interesting to contemplate one of the mild arguments that breaks out during Hitchcock's interview with Truffaut: Truffaut observes the "indirect" sex in Hitchcock's movies, and says that he doubts if the "majority of the public shares your tastes in this matter." Hitchcock seems a bit sensitive to the issue and keeps insisting that his methods are right. "Sex should not be advertized," he says. He prefers English women to Latins because "An English girl, looking like a schoolteacher, is apt to get into a cab with you and, to your surprise, she'll probably pull a man's pants open." In explaining why he usually favors sophisticated blondes, he remarks, "We're after the drawing-room type, the real ladies, who become whores once they're in the bedroom." At an earlier place in the interview, he relates sexual repression to the more general qualities of his films. "Sex on the screen," he says, "must be suspenseful. If sex is too blatant or obvious, there's no suspense."

(It is noteworthy that in *Frenzy,* where at last the treatment of sex is quite explicit, the anxieties of a repressed woman are given one of their most direct representations. Hitchcock shows a buxom, matronly marriage-counsellor being raped by a satyr-like madman. The woman, who has been accused by her ex-husband of being unable to enjoy sex, is trapped in her worst nightmare: as her attacker mutters "lovely, lovely," she grasps the crucifix at her neck and repeats the ninety-first psalm.)

Repression not only has its dramatic uses for Hitchcock, it is also an extension of his personality. He was educated by rather stern Jesuit teachers, and he grew up in a British middle-class culture that did not encourage emotional display. (It was also a culture that gave us popular entertainments like Madame Tussaud's.) He is hardly an adventurous type, having avoided extremes in practically everything except his menu. He lives a quiet, fairly cultivated life, though he loves to tell risqué jokes. He stays removed from Hollywood, and, by his own testimony, he is obsessed with neatness. "I'm full of fears," he tells Truffaut, "and I do my best to avoid complication. . . . I get a feeling of inner peace from a well-organized desk. When I take a bath, I put everything neatly back in place. You wouldn't even know I'd been in the bathroom." Naturally we think of Norman Bates swabbing out the shower, and probably Hitchcock means us to. In the superb sequence where we are shown Norman's efforts to conceal a crime, Hitchcock has given his most concrete demonstration of the tense relationship between order and anxiety; at the same time, he has made a very painful and sly joke about anal-compulsive behavior, a joke that he is strong enough to play at his own expense.

It follows that if Hitchcock's life is well-arranged, so is his work. Though his subject is chaos, he is probably the best-organized movie director who has ever lived and his films give the impression that nothing on the screen was put there by chance. His early training as an engineer and an artist no doubt came to his aid when he began making pictures, enabling him to design and construct his films on a drawingboard before they were ever committed to photography. He is proud of never having to look through a camera once shooting begins, and he barely has to edit his movies at all. John Houseman, the celebrated producer of the Mercury Theatre and the one-time associate of David Selznick, has described Hitchcock as having a "passion for his work, which he approached with an intelligence and an almost scientific clarity to which I was unaccustomed in the theatre." This "scientific" cast of mind allows Hitchcock to develop his cinema from behind a desk, where he works closely with his scriptwriters and sketches out designs for the camera. In a medium which depends more than most upon the accidents of day-to-day circumstances, Hitchcock's methods are unusual; he approaches his craft with the deliberateness of a model builder.

His deliberation reveals itself in the technical expertise of his films, their total command of film grammar. As Andrew Sarris has said, Hitchcock's is "the only contemporary style that unites the divergent classical traditions of Murnau (camera movement) and Eisenstein (montage)." But of these two traditions, it was clearly the latter which influenced Hitchcock most strongly. During the forties he experimented with an expressive tracking style, pushing the experiment to its limits in *Rope* (1948), where he composed an entire film out of ten-minute takes. And yet Hitchcock's camera has never moved in order to "open up" the screen; instead it tries to carry us from one point of interest to another, as in the remarkable tracking shot that concludes the showerbath montage in *Psycho*: We are taken from a close-up of a dead eye, across a room to a close-up of a money-stuffed envelope, and then over to a window for a long shot of a spooky old house. Whether his camera is tracking between compositions or simply cutting, he has always had a

Pavlovian conception of the cinema, creating images strung together in a formula that will excite the audience. That is, he rigorously controls the medium in order to control the psychological responses of his viewers. He frequently describes his control as "pure cinema," which is chiefly a matter of montage. "The point," he says in an early essay about direction, "is to draw the audience right inside the situation instead of leaving them to watch it from outside, from a distance. And you can do this only by breaking the action up into details . . . so that each detail is forced in turn on the attention of the audience and reveals its psychological meaning." Years later, in speaking of *Rear Window,* he remarked, "It represents to me the purest form of cinema, which is called montage: that is, pieces of film put together to make up an idea."

The carefully planned, hence repressive quality of Hitchcock's style makes his visual mannerisms relatively easy to identify. Unlike, say, Orson Welles, who fills every frame with a restless dynamism of form, a whirlwind of movements, Hitchcock gives his images the simplicity and slight unreality of good cartoons, as if the picture had been transformed directly from a line drawing to the screen. He has complained that "most films aren't sufficiently rigorous," because "so few people in the industry know anything about imagery." He is right of course, though one is tempted to argue that not all films should be "rigorous." His own compositions are extremely direct and uncluttered; notice, however, that they are frequently artificial, perhaps because he has sought to impose a mental vision upon a truculent, unyielding reality. Some of the most dramatic moments in his films have a manufactured look: For example, he built a giant toy hand holding a revolver in order to get a close-up down the barrel of a gun in *Spellbound* (1945), and in order to show the face of detective Arbogast falling down the stairs in *Psycho,* he used a tricky process-screen shot. In neither case does the image look real, even if we do not know how the effects were achieved; and yet the scenes work anyway, because they have the clarity and the strangeness of events in a dream.

The "dreamlike" aura of Hitchcock's films has often been noted by his critics. It stems partly from the fetishistic quality of his movies, preoccupied as they are with abnormal behavior in relatively conventional surroundings. His dramatic effects, which have been described as a type of "counterpoint," are actually a skillful bringing-together of repression and fantasy, so that his pictures become unselfconscious enactments of the very process behind dreams. His protagonists frequently enter into situations where subconscious fears and guilts seem to have taken over their waking lives; in the American films especially, one senses a close relationship between the characters' fantasies and the things that happen to them: Joan Fontaine in *Rebecca* and *Suspicion* is a prim, schoolmarmish woman who keeps imagining that her husband is a murderer; Farley Granger in *Strangers on a Train* is a tennis player who would unconsciously like to kill his wife, and then discovers that a psychopath has done the job in his place; Doris Day in *The Man Who Knew Too Much* is a housewife from Indianapolis who has her wish for excitement fulfilled when her child is kidnapped by spies; James Stewart in *Rear Window* is a temporary invalid who enjoys fantasizing about other people's lives, until one of the fantasies comes true. Even the smaller details of Hitchcock's plots are worked out according to the logic of dreams: The incredibly swift transitions that take us from one crisis to another in *Thirty-Nine Steps* and *North by Northwest* have the absurdist dynamics of a nightmare. And consider Hitchcock's preoccupation with doubles or mirror-image relationships, which his French critics have labeled a "transference of guilt": the heroine of *Rebecca* is the "second Mrs. Dewinter," but, unlike the first, is innocent and good; the girl "Charlie" in *Shadow of a Doubt* is the converse of her Uncle Charlie, a wife murderer; Guy in *Strangers on a Train* is the opposite of the psychopath Bruno, but he too has a relative he would like to see dead; the priest in *I Confess* is suspected of a murder because he has a motive and opportunity more valid than the real killer, a man whose confession he has heard; the retired cat-burglar in *To Catch a Thief* is the victim of a female who impersonates him; Manny Baelestro in *The Wrong Man* is the physical double and the moral opposite of the right man; the mysterious female in *Vertigo* has no less than four different manifestations, some of them innocent and some of them evil, so that we can no longer be sure what is reality and what is illusion; Richard Blaney in *Frenzy* is an imbittered, potentially psychotic man whom anyone would think capable of murder—but the crimes of which he is suspected are really committed by his charming, ingratiating friend.

In other words, Hitchcock's movies are something more than "mere" thrillers or disguised morality plays. They work upon us at a particularly intense, immediate level, enacting the fears and desires that run beneath the repressions of ordinary personality. Even his least suspenseful and least successful films, like *The Paradine Case* and *Under Capricorn,* have dealt with the breakdown of civilized restraints and repressions, showing us gentlemen and ladies who, as Hitchcock puts it, "degrade" themselves by falling under the sway of dark passions. Of course there are moral implications in such themes. It should be obvious to anyone who has seen *Psycho* that Hitchcock is aware of the dangers inherent in too much psychological repression; at the same time it should be equally obvious from the quality of his work and his life that he requires a certain orderliness, and that he fears what the loss of order would bring. He has, it seems to me, a conservative and rather pessimistic attitude toward human nature. He is not telling us to liberate ourselves completely; he is allowing us to experience nightmare and dark comedy with a sort of pleasureable uneasiness. He shows us, dispassionately yet often movingly, the paradoxes of guilt and innocence. He is a brilliant social satirist who is fully aware of the tenuousness and occasional absurdity of civilization, but for him there is nothing but chaos and nihilism to offer in its place. That is why his films can offer us witty critiques of society and at the same time never seem especially rebellious or unorthodox. In moving from Britain to America he exchanged a Noel Cowardish, comedy-of-manners surface for a darker, more subtle type of humor, but he has never lost the cool, tongue-in-cheek pose that keeps his work relatively detached. As we might expect, his conventional thrillers are almost entirely free of political tendentiousness; his professional spies are usually insensitive bureaucrats, and it makes very little difference what organization they belong to. (As the chief spy in *North by Northwest* puts it, "The FBI, the CIA, we're all part of the same alphabet soup.") Over against ideologies, Hitchcock depicts human problems, locating his films in a region of the mind, where individuals are beset by social and sexual anxieties.

Of course Hitchcock is a popular filmmaker, and with *Psycho* he desired mainly to stir the emotions of his audience. He achieved that end perfectly, but at the same time he was able to bring to the surface and joke about the underside of American life. Incest, latent homosexuality, voyeurism, necrophilia—all these themes are touched on repeatedly in his American films; in *Psycho* he declares them openly, playing them off against a background of capitalist and puritan repressions. As Professor Leslie Fiedler has shown us (*Love and Death in the American Novel*), such forces have been unconsciously reflected throughout our literature. Hitchcock, however, does not conceal them. In fact, as we shall see, he invites his audience to understand the relationship between their own fantasies and the terror on the screen. He knows that horrors, if properly indulged, can give us satisfaction; but his best films can impress themselves so strongly on our minds that they make us feel less secure, less comfortable with day-to-day existence.

the production

In the interview from which the above remarks are taken, Hitchcock announced to Jean Domarchi and Jean Douchet his plans for a new film, to be called *Psycho*. He explained that he would shoot the picture in Hollywood, where he would construct a gothic mansion and a motel (*"Vous savez ce que c'est qu'un motel?"*) on the vast lots of the old Universal Studios. "*Psycho* will not be a superproduction," he said, "it will be a very strange film in every sense." He planned to work quickly and cheaply because, "in all honesty, I am not at all sure it will be a success. It is very, very out of the ordinary" (my translation).

Of course he was wrong about the box-office potential of the film, which turned out to be one of the top attractions of 1960; *Psycho* cost no more than eight hundred thousand dollars to make, and as of 1967 it had grossed fifteen million dollars. It was, however, "out of the ordinary." It had no major stars in its cast, it was shot in black-and-white, and it told an extremely desolate story with no appealing characterizations. On the other hand, it offered the public a good scare, and it titillated them with sex and violence. A master publicist, Hitchcock assisted in devising advertisements that lured people into the theatre: There were still photos of Janet Leigh in a brassiere, and of Tony Perkins clapping a hand over his mouth in an expression of horror. Hitchcock himself was featured prominently in all the ads, announcing that patrons would not be seated once the film had begun. By this time, thanks to *Alfred Hitchcock Presents,* he was a considerable celebrity, and audiences were given every reason to believe that *Psycho* would be something like the macabre little stories they had been watching at home on Sunday nights.

They were not disappointed. Though *Psycho* transcends the television shows (a few of which Hitchcock actually directed), it was clearly influenced by their format. They were short grisly comedies with ironic, O. Henryesque endings, often closer in spirit to the horror story than to the conventional thriller. They were different from the feature pictures Hitchcock had made before the nineteen fifties, chiefly because they highlighted the pessimistic and even sadistic qualities of his wit—qualities that had been suppressed when his films were produced by other people. In *The Lodger* (1926), he had wanted to leave the audience in doubt as to Ivor Novello's innocence; in *The Secret Agent* (1936), he had wanted to show a scene where Robert Young, a wounded villain, is given a glass of water and then shot to death as he drinks; in *Suspicion* (1941), he had wanted to have Joan Fontaine die of poisoned milk administered by Cary Grant. All these cynical gestures were checked by studio bosses; but for the television series Hitchcock could be as pessimistic as he pleased, probably because he found a charming way to joke about it. Before each program he would appear as master of ceremonies, a portly fellow in a dark business suit, looking like a deadpan cherub. In the measured, distinguished tones of a stuffy English butler, he would welcome his viewers and make absurdly irrelevant commentary on that evening's film; usually he twitted the sponsors, and his audience loved it. He was pleasantly iconoclastic, his witticisms and his bland appearance putting the grimmer aspects of the stories at a safe distance. Though unconventional, the stories themselves were never really antisocial; in fact, one might say that they were both nasty and oddly moral. As Andrew Sarris and several other commentators have observed, Hitchcock is no anarchist. His villains are often sympathetic, yet they are inevitably trapped by an unremitting, almost cosmic system of justice. Nevertheless, since the early fifties Hitchcock's work in television and in the movies proper had grown slightly more depressing, his protagonists more guilt-ridden. *The Wrong Man, Vertigo,* and *The Birds* have downbeat, ambiguous endings, unrelieved by humor; and *Psycho* is in some ways the bleakest show of them all, although it entertains us with the surprises and the sardonic wit that had made Hitchcock's television program a great success.

In many respects, *Psycho* even has the same "look" as one of the television films, chiefly because all the interiors were filmed at Revue Studios using the same facilities as *Alfred Hitchcock Presents*. True to his promise, Hitchcock shot the picture on a rapid schedule, forsaking his regular associate, Robert Burks, in favor of John Russell, the chief cameraman on the television series. Burks, Hitchcock explained, was too slow and meticulous, whereas Russell was an exceedingly fast, high-quality craftsman. (Previously, he had helped create the brilliant *mise-en-scène* for Samuel Fuller's quicky production of *Park Row*.) The choice turned out to be a wise one; using the simplest techniques and the basic contrasts of black-and-white photography, Russell achieved superb effects, and was nominated for the 1960 Academy Award.

On the other hand, several members of the production staff were veterans of Hitchcock's major films. George Tomasini had been his editor since 1954, and Saul Bass, the title designer, had created the remarkable graphics for *Vertigo* and *North by Northwest*. Among this group of assistants, musical director Bernard Herrmann deserves special attention; he composed music for most of the late Hitchcock features, giving them a large measure of their strange, almost otherworldly atmosphere. (He is paid a sort of tribute in the American version of *The Man Who Knew Too Much*, where he conducts the orchestra in the Albert Hall sequence and has his name displayed in big letters on posters advertising the concert.) A serious musician who has divided his career between America and England, Herrmann began contributing to the popular arts in the thirties, when he was hired as the boy conductor of the CBS radio orchestra. He directed the music for Orson Welles' *Mercury Theatre of the Air* and later came to Hollywood to compose the score for *Citizen Kane*. His collaboration was especially important to Hitchcock, who uses a considerable amount of music but avoids anything that could be called a "tuneful" background. Since he first experimented with talkies, Hitchcock has tried to have the soundtrack of his pictures function in a relatively abstract way, counterpointing or commenting upon the imagery; thus, when he came to make *The Birds,* which uses no music, he hired Herrmann as a "sound consultant" to orchestrate noises and bird calls. For *Psycho,* Herrmann's work was simple but apt: he composed a few recurring motifs which add enormously to the impact of the film— consider, for example, the shrilling violin that accompanies Mrs. Bates' attacks. (Interestingly enough, Herrmann says that when he first saw *Psycho,* he was told *not* to compose music for the stab- bings. Only later, when Hitchcock felt disappointed with the fin- ished film, was the stunning murder music added. Hitchcock, need- less to say, was delighted.)

For the script of *Psycho,* much credit should go to Hitchcock, though Joseph Stephano is listed as the single writer. Usually, Hitch- cock works on a screenplay by providing his writers with the gen- eral shape of a story, letting his visual ideas dictate the content. As Raymond Chandler once observed, Hitchcock "directs a film in his head before he knows what the story is. . . . I guess that's why some of his pictures lose their grip on logic." Of course Hitchcock is pro- foundly indifferent to the logic of conventional realism, since he wants to deal in sharp visual contrasts and absurdist situations. In *Psycho,* he clearly had in mind a contrast between the painfully ordinary, depressing life of Marion Crane, and the baroque, night- marish world of Norman Bates—the motel *vs.* the Gothic mansion. At almost every level, *Psycho* is given energy by what Andrew Sar- ris has called "counterpoint": Norman's psychosis is set off against the sweetness of Fairvale, the brutal murder is staged in a white- tiled shower, etc. Moreover, these contrasts, which are the whole basis of the film, were only barely suggested by Hitchcock's source, a pot-boiler novel by Robert Bloch.

Bloch has subsequently gone on to write several movies in the *Psycho* vein, working for a time with Hammer Films, the English studio which revitalized the contemporary horror picture. He is still remembered occasionally as the "author" of *Psycho,* but in every sense Hitchcock and Stephano's version of the story is better. The novel is set entirely in a midwestern town called Fairvale. It opens by introducing Norman Bates, a plump, balding, middle- aged fellow who wears rimless glasses and keeps a stuffed squirrel in the kitchen of the old Victorian house where he lives. Norman drinks a good deal, and he has none of the boyish pleasantness of a Tony Perkins. Much of the novel is told from his point of view, and conversations between him and his mother are reported as if they were actually happening. The story of "Mary" Crane (later we will discuss why Hitchcock changed her name) is given in a brief, largely expository flashback which explains how she came to steal forty thousand dollars from a real-estate office in Texas. She arrives at the Bates Motel at the beginning of the novel; Norman checks her in and then peeks at her through a hole drilled behind the framed license in his office. Mary strips, does a playful, utterly gratuitous bump-and-grind before a mirror in her room, and takes a shower. A few moments pass, and a grotesquely made-up old woman enters the motel bathroom, cutting the girl's head off with one neat stroke. From this point, the plot of the novel is nearly the same as the second half of Hitchcock's film, though it differs in some important details: Arbogast, the private eye, is killed with a razor when he enters the front door of the Bates' house. Later, Lila Crane (new romantic interest for Sam Loomis, a shy, retiring type who loves classical music) investigates the old house during a thunderstorm. She visits Norman's room first of all, and finds it not nearly so strange as the one in the film; ultimately, Norman's secret is discovered, and in the epilogue his behavior is "explained" through a conversation between Sam and Lila. We are told that a psychiatrist named Steiner has identified Norman as a transvestite and a psychotic schizophrenic. The book ends with "Norma" Bates talking to herself in a barred room, swearing that she wouldn't even harm a fly.

Bloch's novel is a pretty vulgar piece of writing, and it is surprising that Hitchcock could have seen so many possibilities in the story. There is nothing in Bloch's prose even roughly to approximate the technical brilliance of the film, and though Joseph Stephano's dialogue is fairly ordinary—the movie is almost half silent —it is at least better than the original. Generally speaking, Hitchcock and Stephano tried to avoid cliché; even when they used the stock paraphernalia of the horror picture, they did so with a wry intelligence that brings new life to a dead genre. Perhaps the most interesting of the many changes they made was in the overall structure of the book. They elaborated the "Mary" Crane story, giving the film a double plot, and not introducing Norman Bates until the picture was a third over. Obviously, Hitchcock wanted to throw the audience so much off guard that the shower murder would come as the greatest shock effect in the history of cinema; equally important, the formal balancing of two stories would give the film a special richness. The lives of Marion Crane and Norman Bates, when set off against one another, produce a fascinating web of comparisons and contrasts which gains in significance with every viewing; what is more, the relationship between these characters is felt chiefly at the *visual* level, where Hitchcock's style transforms a pulp story into a masterpiece of "pure" filmmaking.

These matters, however, are best dealt with in the next section, where the themes and the technical excellence of *Psycho* can be analysed in more detail. The sources and the production facilities of the film were modest, but the results were something else again.

analysis

The opening sequences of *Psycho,* like nearly everything else in the film, bear testimony to a careful preplanning. They have a deliberateness, a rhythm and logic that could only have been worked out in advance.

After the credits, there is a dissolve to a view of city rooftops; the sun is bright, and in the distance we can see a desert landscape half-obscured by haze. The camera is panning slowly, pointed first at a prosperous part of town, where a new building is under construction. As the camera eye roves across a thoroughfare, an almost imperceptible dissolve takes us to a slightly closer view. At the same time, words in small block capitals appear at either side of the screen and converge: PHOENIX, ARIZONA. The camera is still panning slowly to the right, and we begin to see a rather drab block of buildings on the other side of town; another set of titles converges at the center—FRIDAY, DECEMBER ELEVENTH—and another dissolve takes us a bit closer. The panning movement continues, but now the camera begins a slow zoom down toward one of the buildings, and a last title appears: TWO FORTY-THREE P.M. Still another dissolve, and the camera stops before an ugly-looking wall, peering down at a bank of windows. Slowly, it moves toward the single opening, where a set of closed and lowered venetian blinds has left about six inches of space. Cut to a closer view of the window (a stage set); the camera slides toward the murky opening under the blinds, and enters a room.

The bright sun on the windowsill has made us unaccustomed to the light inside. At first there is only inky darkness, but as the camera pans to the right, with the same speed as before, we can make out a few blurred objects. Now we begin to see clearly: We stop at the foot of an iron bedstead in a dingy hotel room. A shirtless man is standing beside the bed, his head out of our view, and a girl (Janet Leigh) is lying down, looking up at him. She wears a half-slip; we see her slender legs and her face beyond a mountainous white brassiere. "Never did eat your lunch, did you?" the man's voice says. Cut to a close-up of a depressing tableau on a scarred little table: a hotel water pitcher with several glasses, a soft-drink bottle, a paper cup, and an uneaten sandwich in waxed paper. "I've got to get back to the office," the girl replies.

Even in these first moments Hitchcock's typical mannerisms are revealed, together with some echoes, perhaps unintentional, of his earlier work. For example, the titles are similar to the ones he used a year before, in a short television film called "Banquo's Chair," which opens with the camera travelling across a row of buildings and moving in toward a doorway while words announce an exact place, date, and time. "Banquo's Chair" is set in Edwardian England, in an elegant Mayfair apartment, and it concerns the appearance of a ghost; the titles at the opening are tongue-in-cheek, but they also have a function similar to the conventional "framing" device in tales like *The Ancient Mariner* or *Turn of the Screw,* giving a realistic starting ground from which to depart into fantasy and terror. In *Psycho,* as in "Banquo's Chair," we are given a factual opening for a story that will eventually turn into Gothic horror. Why Phoenix, why two forty-three p.m.? There are some immediate reasons— Phoenix, after all, is the name of a bird, and *Psycho* is full of bird references; two forty-three is a way of reminding us, as Hitchcock does in his interview with Truffaut, that "this is the only time the poor girl has to go to bed with her lover." But perhaps more important is the manipulative logic of beginning on a witty, quasi-documentary note, so that the horror-movie iconography in the later sequences will come upon us with a greater shock, disturbing our excessively secure relationship to ordinary life. As we shall see, the film is structured by the elemental contrasts in its settings, as if to emphasize the disparity between reality and nightmare. The first part is designed to present a mundane, daytime world which is fraught with barely repressed tensions; later, when the characters are shown in the grip of neurosis or psychosis, the ordinary exterior will give way to darkness, and ultimately to the fantastic shadows of an isolated Victorian house. Significantly, once the horror begins, *Psycho* will give less attention to factual details. A little over half of the story will take place in an archetypal though somewhat anachronistic American town with the ironic name, "Fairvale."

The opening camera movement from a panoramic view of a city down to an open window operates on what Truffaut calls the "farthest to the nearest" principle, a vivid expository device that one can find in most of Hitchcock's films. There is a very similar shot at the opening of his wartime spy thriller, *Foreign Correspondent* (1940), where we close in on a skyscraper and move directly into an office; and in *Frenzy* (1972) Hitchcock takes us swooping down upon London, beneath Tower bridge, until we discover a body floating in the Thames. But in *Psycho,* the first few images have more than expository value. They take us from surfaces to depths; from daylight to a sinister, murky darkness; from the most public view to the most intimate—thus announcing the movement of the film as a whole. Notice, too, that the opening shot is explicitly voyeuristic, the camera inviting the audience to become "peepers." Hitchcock knows that our relationship to the figures on a movie screen is different from our relationship to characters in a play or a novel; in fact it is significant that in *Rear Window* and *Psycho,* his two most "purely cinematic" works, he enjoys drawing a parallel between voyeurs on the screen and voyeurs in the audience. When Truffaut asks whether the James Stewart character in *Rear Window,* who spends the entire movie looking in other people's windows, is "merely curious," Hitchcock answers, "He's a real peeping Tom . . . he's a snooper, but aren't we all?" Indeed we are. In *Psycho,* when we peek in through a window and discover half-naked bodies, we are enjoying an act which will later be duplicated by Norman Bates, who peers through a tiny hole to watch Marion Crane take a shower. In this respect as in several others, Hitchcock gives us ironic reminders of the first line between normal and abnormal behavior; he implicates his audience (himself as well) and he suggests that his conception of "pure film" is far from an empty formalism.

But if the opening shots remind us of other Hitchcock films, the grittiness of the *mise-en-scène,* the relative starkness of the black-and-white photography, and above all the blatantly exposed flesh are atypical. The hotel room where Sam Loomis and Marion Crane make love is utterly barren, and Hitchcock and his photographer John Russell have generally avoided opportunities for dramatic visuals. For example, it has become a cliché of black-and-white movies to use venetian blinds to throw expressive shadows on the walls, but in the opening of *Psycho* the blinds are always lowered or pulled up, so that the room is either dim or washed with a bright, flat light. The walls are dirty, blank, a testimony to the impoverished, unhappy nature of the love affair. The drab atmosphere is almost like a parody of the popular American notion of a late-fifties foreign movie, which was supposed to mingle sex with social realism; and it is an atmosphere particularly uncharacteristic of this phase in Hitchcock's career. Since the middle fifties, he and Robert Burks, his chief cameraman, had developed a sensitive and beautiful color photography, which achieved its fullest expression in *Vertigo* (1958). The opening parts of *Psycho* offer a completely different visual experience, more like an elaborate version of Hitchcock and Russell's black-and-white TV shows. *Psycho* is a funky-looking movie, and it is precisely this funkyness that evokes so much praise from a critic like Manny Farber, who loves the way the first half of the picture evokes "the humdrum day-in-the-life-of a real estate receptionist."

Farber calls *Psycho* "Godardlike" in its fascination with bare, anonymous rooms; but on the other hand the actual staging of the love scene, the choreography of the camera and actors, is pure Hitchcock. We see Sam Loomis (John Gavin) move down to the bed as Marion Crane sits up; their bodies are nicely composed, like an erotic sculpture, and as they kiss they form a soft triangle of flesh against the dark walls. The camera moves in on them as they embrace and lie down together. They kiss each other softly, repeatedly, talking all the while, their bodies turning on the bed. While they caress, the camera begins drifting to the right, circling the two figures until it has gone halfway around the room. Since *Notorious* in 1946 Hitchcock has employed these same techniques again and again; roughly similar scenes can be found in *Rear Window, To Catch a Thief, Vertigo,* and *North by Northwest,* where passion is nearly always repressed, communicated not by wrestling and heavy breathing, but by soft, teasing caresses and gentle kisses. In the typical Hitchcock love scene, the actors' movements are usually counterpointed by a low-voiced conversation about some banal issue (in *Notorious,* it was dishwashing and chicken dinner); as they talk, they brush against each other's lips, their bodies revolving in a slow dance, the camera sometimes gliding around them. In *Psycho,* Sam and Marion talk about the hot weather, about meeting in dreary hotels, about all the frustrations of their love life. (Some of the dialog is slyly ironic: "Hotels of this sort aren't interested in you when you come in," she says, "but when your time is up. . . ." The full meaning of such a remark is not obvious when we first see the film, but on subsequent viewings, when we know what will happen at the Bates' motel, it strikes us as a grisly foreshadowing.) Notice, too, that the gliding, encircling movement of the camera is once again an implicit recognition of the audience's erotic desires. Hitchcock acknowledges such an implication in his interview with Truffaut, where he says that in filming the famous love scene for *Notorious,* he felt "the public, represented by the camera, was the third party to this embrace."

After several moments, the lovers part. Marion rises from the bed, and as she does so, Hitchcock cuts to a long shot (typically, he will have the actor move before a cut, his camera never anticipating an action). Marion crosses, circling the room until she stands at the left of the frame, facing our direction, where she begins to dress. Until this point, we have been intensely aware of her semi-nudity, especially her white brassiere. As I have said, such forthright exposure of sex is a rarity in Hitchcock's films. One thinks of Robert Donat's hand manacled to Madeline Carroll as she removes her stockings in *The Thirty-Nine Steps,* or of the sensuality that the presence of Kim Novak imparts to *Rear Window*; but generally, except in *Frenzy,* Hitchcock has liked to keep sex well covered-up. In fact, for *Torn Curtain,* made at the start of the nudity vogue, he intentionally staged a love scene in a freezing cold ship's cabin, showing Paul Newman and Julie Andrews in bed with all their clothes on, huddled under heavy blankets. In *Psycho,* by contrast, the half-slip and the massive brassiere become obsessive images. In the first half of the picture we see Janet Leigh in this costume no less than three times, and Hitchcock's advertising campaign for *Psycho* featured a still photo of her seated on a bed in a bra, her body turned slightly to make the breasts stand out. Obviously Hitchcock was capitalizing on the voyeurism of his audience and preparing them to sympathize with Norman Bates' peeking; but he also had another, less immediately apparent motive. As Raymond Durgnat has observed, *Psycho* is in part a "derisive misuse of the key images of the American way of life: Momism (but it blames son), cash (and rural virtue), necking (and respectability), plumbing and smart cars." The only thing missing from Durgnat's list, though it is implied by "Momism," is the brassiere, the emblem of breast fetishism. Thus Janet Leigh's frail body and her extremely large and beautiful breasts are elements in a subtle, macabre joke, a devilish satire. If we are not aware of this at first, it is because Hitchcock's wit is always understated; he avoids those obtrusive pokes in the ribs that one can find everywhere in a film like *Lolita,* and he displays a finer intelligence than most satirists with greater reputations.

In choosing Janet Leigh and Tony Perkins for the lead roles, Hitchcock also demonstrated his gift for casting. They give the best performances of their careers, but it is clear that they were chosen mainly for physical and emotional properties they would naturally bring to their parts. In the case of Janet Leigh, there is something diabolical about Hitchcock's selection, which makes us feel uncomfortable even while we applaud its aptness. To begin with, she is a star, and the audience will not expect her to be killed off before the movie is half over; on the other hand, she is not too big a star, so Hitchcock can get away with it. She is a blonde, like all his heroines, and both she and Perkins have slender bodies which augment the bird-motif—in fact, Leigh's bird-like shape is entirely in keeping with the name of the character she plays, and with Norman Bates' hobby of killing and stuffing birds. Finally, of course, there is her considerable sex appeal, which previously had been used effectively by only two other directors: Joseph von Sternberg in *Jet Pilot* (produced in the early fifties by Howard Hughes, again indulging his penchant for airplanes and big breasts), and Orson Welles in *Touch of Evil* (1958). Probably Hitchcock did not see *Jet Pilot,* where Leigh was cast in a silly if highly erotic role; but it would be interesting to know if he saw the Welles film, which shows her in scanty lingerie and makes her the victim of rape in a motel room. No matter how he came to think of her, she is an ideal choice to play

Marion Crane, whose breasts are especially desirable to a psycho-path with an unnatural love for his mother. Then, too, she has aged just enough; her body has grown thinner, her face taken on a hard-edged, slightly mocking intelligence that is perfectly appropriate for a secretary who has been treated a bit roughly and has begun to long for security.

We become aware of her plight as the scene in the hotel room progresses. She has told Sam that this will be the last time for them to meet over a lunch hour; she wants him to come home with her, to meet her sister, to behave with "respectability." Her tone is neither shrewish nor puritanical, it is merely the voice of what Hitchcock has called an "ordinary bourgeois," a girl who is weary of her lot. As she talks, Sam rises and sits in a chair across the room, putting on his shirt. Hitchcock cuts back and forth between close-ups of the two, suggesting the barrier that has risen between them. Sam jokes about the burdens of respectability, complaining about his dead father's debts and his ex-wife's alimony. Marion interrupts to remind him that "they also pay who meet in hotel rooms," and he crosses to embrace her again, their faces somewhat romantically framed by soft light from an expanse of closed venetian blinds. Marion wants to be his wife, no matter what, but he says that he cannot ask her to live behind a hardware store (meeting in a cheap hotel has not seemed to bother him). Finally he moves away, back to his corner, where he raises the blinds and stares morosely out the window. The light makes us more aware of the ugly walls and a few other details: a black electric fan, a beaten chest of drawers, a piece of junk pottery. The scene ends with Marion's problem un-resolved. "Don't miss your plane," she tells Sam. She pecks him on the cheek, wistfully reminding him to put his shoes on, and then leaves for work.

A dissolve takes us to the Lowrey Real Estate offices. The set is lighter, more comfortable than the hotel room we have just left, but it is far from luxurious. Two secretaries work together in the ante-room, without benefit of the air-conditioning their employer has in-stalled in his own office. There are several furnishings, a big iron safe in the corner, some plotted plants, and a series of pictures on the walls, including an enormous photograph of a desert landscape directly behind Marion's desk. Hitchcock's style is utilitarian; the sequence was obviously filmed quickly, with few set-ups and no unusual camera angles or extreme close-ups. At one point, Vaughn Taylor, the actor playing Mr. Lowrey, calls the second secretary in the office "Marion," confusing her with the Janet Leigh character— later we discover that her name is supposed to be "Carolyn." Either Hitchcock was so uninterested that he did not notice, or in his desire to save money he was content to let the error pass.

At the beginning of the scene, Marion Crane is walking anxiously through the door, asking her coworker if the boss is back from lunch yet. Outside the office window we see Hitchcock himself, in a stetson, waiting for a bus. In fact, the other secretary is played by his daughter Pat, a chubby girl who had previously appeared in *Strangers on a Train* as the near victim of a homicidal maniac. Here, as in the earlier film, she is effective in a comic but unpleasant role—a chattering, whiny-voiced brat, newly married, who gives repulsive details about her sex life. "Have you got a headache?" she asks, looking at Marion's drawn face, and then babbling on: "I've got something—not aspirin. My mother's doctor gave them to me the day of my wedding." She grins. "Teddy was furious when he found out I'd taken tranquilizers." Marion asks if there have been any calls. "Teddy called—me. My mother called to see if Teddy called. . . . Oh yes, your sister called to say she'd be in Tucson over the weekend." As the scene develops, these openly satiric details will function to increase our sympathy for Marion. She is surrounded by vulgar, undeserving types who have marriage, money, and sometimes both. When the boss returns from lunch accompanied by Mr. Cassady, a drunken oilman, her headache is exacerbated. Cassady (Frank Albertson) wears a cowboy hat, like his namesake. He slides one haunch up on Marion's desk and leans down to leer at her, remarking that he has just bought an expensive piece of property for his daughter: "Tomorrow's the day my sweet little girl—oh not you, my daughter, my baby—stands her sweet self up there and gets married away from me." Everything he says makes us feel the basic injustice of Marion's situation. "I want you to take a look at my baby," he says, drawing out a photo. "Eighteen years old, and she never had an unhappy day in any one of those years." Leaning still closer, he mutters in a boozy voice, "You know what I do about unhappiness? I buy it off. Are you unhappy?" He pulls out forty thousand dollars and waves it under Marion's nose, boasting "I never carry more than I can afford to lose." The other secretary is overcome: "I declare!" she says. "I don't," the oilman chuckles. "That's how I get to keep it."

After this, we are ready to accept Marion's decision to steal the money, even though her behavior has been summarily motivated and seems to run against the grain of her character. We know, by the logic of the movies and by the logic of her situation, that she will never get away with it. She has stepped into what she will later call a "trap," and her headache is only the preliminary to a deepening neurosis, a compulsion that will lead her toward the world of Norman Bates. Notice, too, as a further preliminary to Norman's half of the film, that the opening scenes have been filled with references to parents and children. In changing Robert Bloch's novel by greatly expanding the story of the runaway secretary, Hitchcock and his screenwriter Joseph Stephano sought to unify their double plot by comparisons and contrasts. As Robin Wood has pointed out, the "normal" characters we meet in the first few minutes are nearly all victims of parents or victimizers of children. Sam Loomis must pay off his dead father's debts; Marion Crane, whose parents are also dead, must work and live with her younger sister (Sam jokes that if they make love at her house, they will have to "turn mother's picture to the wall"). The secretary in Marion's office is the favorite child of a clinging mother; the oilman thinks he will buy happiness for his "sweet little girl." All these references to "family drama" help prepare us for Norman Bates and his mother, revealing once more the narrow line between sanity and madness. Just as the audience, through its desires and sympathies, is slightly complicit in the guilt of Marion and Norman, so the "normal" characters are barely separated from the "abnormal" ones.

As the scene in the real estate office ends, Marion's boss nervously tells her to put the forty thousand dollars in a safe deposit box at the bank until his client sobers up. She stuffs the money in an envelope, and, pleading her headache, asks for the rest of the afternoon off. As she is about to leave, we see her in close-up. "Aren't you going to take the pills?" the other secretary asks. "No," Marion answers, smiling faintly, "you can't buy off unhappiness with pills." She is, however, ready to buy off her problems with stolen money, and the photo of a desert on the wall behind her suggests the consequences.

When we next see Marion, she is at home: the camera stands at eye level, looking across a neatly made bed at an open closet. The room is small and rather gray, with a feminine decor; again we are reminded of parents and children by the pictures of infants and relatives all around. Marion walks into the frame, now wearing a black brassiere—Hitchcock's playful way of indicating her new life as a thief. She moves toward her closet, turning and glancing uneasily down at something. As she slips off her shoes and chooses a dress, the camera tilts down to reveal that she has not deposited the forty thousand dollars: the stuffed envelope lies on the bed. Now the camera dollys in to a giant close-up of the money, and Bernard Herrmann's music begins to play a slow theme in a minor key, counterpointed with a high-pitched woodwind passage which has the rhythm of a nervous pulse. The camera slides across the bed to the left, and we see Marion's suitcase, opened and loaded with clothes.

Here, at a crucial juncture in the plot, Hitchcock's camera calls attention to itself by moving independently of any action on the screen. As in the opening shots, which also involved a half-dressed Janet Leigh, we are made slightly aware of ourselves watching a movie. The point of view is shifted; Marion has her back turned, and Hitchcock reminds us that we are interlopers. He also breaks, if only for a moment, what Henry James liked to call the "illusion of reality," the feeling that events are being presented neutrally, without an author pulling strings. In the previous sequence his technique was straightforward and relatively self-effacing (though he appeared briefly on the screen in one of his typical walk-ons). We were made to sympathize with Marion, and if we did not actually look through her eyes, we were shown events as they would impinge on her consciousness. Here, where the camera moves down to peep at objects in the room while she is looking the other way, our whole relationship to events on the screen changes; we are once again conscious of our voyeurism, and at the same time we become aware of Alfred Hitchcock, the authorial intelligence who controls what we see. This is not to say we lose interest in the story—surely we are intrigued by the discovery of the envelope, excited a little by Herrmann's dramatic music—but the tiny camera movement creates an ironic distance, much like a comment by the storyteller.

There are directors and critics who dislike even such modestly obtrusive effects; yet when most people see a Hitchcock film they enjoy being reminded that he is there. He has made himself a personality, a clever raconteur who amuses us with outright declarations of his presence. Of course he knows when to reveal himself and when to be silent, so that his films typically move back and forth between lucid narration and *tour de force*. Sometimes, when we feel his presence most openly, as in the magnificent crop-dusting montage of *North by Northwest,* the suspense he generates is intimately bound up with our acknowledgment of his visual wit. At other times, as in the slow, silent passage of a camera down an empty stairway in *Frenzy,* we are frozen by pity and terror, and the director becomes a poetic commentator. Even so, in his later films Hitchcock has cultivated a relatively "invisible" camera style, in which even the most radically unusual camera angles are designed to serve the emotional effects of the story. Indeed, he has been critical of techniques that call attention to themselves. For example, in his interview with Peter Bogdanovitch, he seems apologetic about the elaborate tracking in the pictures he made during the forties: "I don't think it was really right," he says, "because, after all, the eye must look at the character. It must not be conscious of a camera dollying unless you are dollying or zooming in for a particular purpose." In *Psycho,* as we shall see, there is nearly always a "particular purpose," part of it being that Hitchcock wants to make us aware of our role as spectators. His movie is in many ways about the act of watching; it is "pure cinema" not only because of its visual power, but also because it invites us, in relatively unobtrusive ways, to contemplate our relationship to the medium. When we first see the film we are innocent, not recognizing these implications of the style; we are, in the words of Leo Braudy, an "irresponsible audience." Though we are slyly teased about our voyeurism, we remain complacent. Finally, as Braudy says, we will be made to go through the "punishment of terror."

In the brief sequence where Marion prepares to run away, the camera detaches itself only once, briefly turning the audience into snoopers; after she puts her dress on, the camera becomes invisible again, moving only slightly to keep her in view as she walks about the room. She tries to avoid the money, but her glance keeps turning compulsively toward it, and each time she looks at the bed Hitchcock cuts to a close-up of the envelope, showing it from her perspective. He is, of course, a master at using subjective camera angles to give psychological intensity to his narratives, and usually the effect he produces is disturbing, even magical. It is a paradox that the awkwardness of the subjective camera should come to his aid in these moments. Anyone who has seen Robert Montgomery's experiments with a purely subjective style in *Lady in the Lake* (1946) will understand how unconvincing the movie camera becomes when it pretends to be a character. The lens of a camera cannot "see" in the same way as a human eye; as a result, an essentially realistic film like Montgomery's is totally destroyed by the technique. (Truffaut has observed that to be truly subjective, the movie camera should usually be pointed *toward* the characer, so that we see his reactions, not the things he is looking at.) Notice that Hitchcock conserves his subjective angles for moments of extreme psychological tension, when the slightly distorted, unrealistic effect will express a character's anxiety. In looking through the eyes of his protagonists, we have the feeling that the most commonplace scenes are alien, terrifying. This is the first instance of the method in *Psycho,* and it is a fairly minor one; but from now until Marion's death we will repeatedly see things from her vantage point, until the environment becomes demonic. Hitchcock allows us to share her insecurities, so that we will be devastated by her murder. He also lets us understand what it is like to become almost mad.

The repeated subjective views give the stuffed envelope a sinister, anthropomorphic quality; we watch Marion yielding to the money even while she tries to avoid it. She buttons her dress and slips on her shoes, her glance falling inadvertently down. (As she moves a bit to the left, still looking at the money, we can see over her shoulder an open bathroom door and a shower spigot—another of those grisly foreshadowings that escape us entirely the first time we view the film.) She puts a few more items into the suitcase, crosses to the left, and looks hard at herself in a mirror. (She will repeatedly encounter mirrors, but this is the last time she will be able to confront her own gaze.) Slowly her head turns and she looks over her shoulder toward the bed. She puts a few more items into the case and slips a file containing her auto registration into her purse. As she closes the suitcase, she again finds herself staring at the envelope. She crosses, sits on the bed, and then, almost without looking, slips the stolen money into her purse. The sequence ends as she picks up her coat and suitcase and leaves the room.

For the next fourteen minutes, we are given a detailed account of Marion's flight from Phoenix, an episode that Robert Bloch's novel mentions in a few paragraphs. It contains some of the most impressive passages in all of Hitchcock's work, but it is not simply a beautiful conception which can be lifted out of context for our admiration. Among others things, it is a brilliant transition between the two "worlds" of the film. On the one hand is Marion's relatively normal if barren life as a receptionist, presented largely through a series of gray, unemphatic settings—the beat-up hotel room where she has a love affair, the real estate office where she works, and the small bedroom where she lives. On the other hand is the decidedly abnormal life of Norman Bates, the sexual psychopath who surrounds himself with stuffed birds of prey and lives in a huge Victorian house atop a hill. The Marion Crane story involves the city, the America of the fast buck; the Norman Bates story involves the country, the America of "rural virtue" and sexual repressions. The difference between these two words is roughly the difference between the Bates motel and the massive Gothic building behind it, or, as many critics have observed, between a film by Godard and a film by James Whale. *Psycho* is all the more remarkable for the way it plays these entirely different modes off against one another without falling apart, as if to suggest a relationship between daytime Americana and a night world of baroque terror.

Marion Crane herself tells us at a later point that her attempt to steal forty thousand dollars is a temporary insanity; therefore the images in this section of the film are designed to present a gradual breakdown of psychological control, a descent into terror. Hitchcock does not allow us to pass too quickly from one realm to the other, and yet one cannot help but be impressed by the classically simple and straightforward means by which he creates a growing paranoia and desperation. We first see Marion in a close-up as she sits behind the wheel of her car. (In fact, the major part of what

follows will be made up of a simple cutting back and forth between
her face and the road ahead.) Her mouth is set, her eyes staring
grimly. She is imagining Sam's voice, which we hear over the soundtrack: "Marion . . . what are you doing up here?" She looks uneasy
and grips the wheel, trying to shake off the thought as her car comes
to a stop at a traffic light. From her perspective, we see pedestrians
crossing. Down the avenue we can make out Christmas decorations,
another of the film's incongruities—the date, we remember, is December eleventh, but the weather in Phoenix is very hot, and the
atmosphere in the rest of the picture will be more appropriate to
Halloween. Several people go past, and then we see Marion's boss
with his oilman client, the first of the bad omens which will intensify
her fear. She gives an uneasy smile and waves; the boss stops on a
corner, turns, frowns, then moves slowly on without speaking. The
light has changed and Marion drives ahead, her eyes anxious, as
Bernard Herrmann's pounding theme music begins. She takes one
uneasy glance over her shoulder and keeps driving.

The image dissolves to the first in a series of extraordinarily sad,
colorless landscapes seen from the window of the moving car. Time
has passed, and the sun is going down. Above is a stream of darken-
ing clouds, below, on the horizon, a few black telephone poles, some
ugly looking shrubs, and the flashing lights of an occasional car.
Another dissolve, and we see an extreme close-up of Marion's face.
Until now the camera has kept at a relative distance, allowing her
hands and shoulders into the frame, but here it is set very close, as
if to underline the fatigue in her eyes. We cut back to a view of the
highway; night has fallen, and a steady stream of traffic goes by, the
lights making bright, hypnotic patterns, the road nearly invisible.
We return to Marion's face, her eyes squinting in the glare of headlights. The tempo of the editing has accelerated with her mounting
discomfort, and now the screen fades to blackness as Herrmann's
music slows and dies.

The next scene has a fairly simple content: In broad daylight on
a deserted road we discover Marion's car, pulled off to the side.
A patrol cars passes, stops, backs up, and parks. A policeman
(Mort Mills) gets out, wakes the sleeping Marion, and questions
her. She is terrified and manages to arouse his suspicion by her

nervous, defensive behavior. Finally the policeman lets her go and she drives on, glancing nervously into her rear-view mirror.

In the hands of most filmmakers, such an episode would be as flat as it sounds on paper, but Hitchcock makes it an indelible moment, an achievement of what one is tempted to call "pure cinema," if the term did not seem to indicate a merely formal beauty. Our relationship to the images is kinetic; we cannot watch them with a detached, rarified, purely aesthetic gratification, because the man who questions Marion Crane is more than just an ordinary cop. Hitchcock has invested his implacable countenance with the power of a symbol; as he looks in the car we feel a psychic menace, a terror that is somehow moral. If *The Wrong Man* gives a more sustained presentation of Hitchcock's celebrated fear of lawmen, a few images from *Psycho* leave us with a stronger impression.

The effectiveness of this sequence, its power of sticking in one's mind, lies in the absolute simplicity of its design. It opens with an evocative landscape, one of those bright, rather pleasant settings that heighten menace by their incongruity. The screen lightens to show a nearly deserted road. In the background, rising from left to right, we see a grassy hillside; the sky is white, and the land seems dry and empty, except for a flowered shrub in the left foreground waving slightly in the breeze. In the distance, a bit off center, we see Marion's car pulled off the road, a stark black telephone pole rising behind it and almost cutting the screen in half. The patrol car drives past, stops, and then backs up to park. We cut to a view from the roadside, looking down the side of Marion's car toward the policeman as he gets out and walks forward. The white road, lined with telephone poles and fenceposts, threads off into rolling hills. The tall shape of the policeman is silhouetted, but as he walks forward we can see him more clearly—he is a big, handsome, broad-shouldered fellow with the typical stormtrooper uniform of a highway cop.

Except for a brief insert of a license plate a bit later on, these two shots are the only parts of the sequence which were filmed outdoors. Everything else was done in the studio, using back projection, and the result is a sudden movement from the real to the artificial. In most films the intrusion of studio mechanics would be awkward, but here once again a certain artificiality works in Hitchcock's favor. The close-ups, with the actors' faces set off against projected backgrounds, have the impact of cartoons; they are stylized, as if to suggest the distorted psychological intensity the moment has for Marion. The policeman, seen from Marion's point of view in an enormous close-up, is like something in a dream: His face is poked up close to the window, occupying most of the frame; behind him the sky is white, bare. His visor is pulled down and his eyes are obscured by sunglasses as dark as a blind man's. He is utterly expressionless—at first glance his head looks like a giant mask.

Terrified, Marion's first impulse is to start the car, but the policeman stops her. She rolls down the window and for the next few lines of dialog Hitchcock cuts back and forth between close-ups, Marion seen from a slightly high angle, the policeman from a very close, subjective vantage, so that he might be looking at us. Until this point, Hitchcock has been sparing of extreme close-ups. Only once before, in the last shot of Marion's fatigue-ridden eyes as she drove her car through the night, has the camera been so near to an actor. Hitchcock believes that a movie is made from faces, but he has also said that "the size of an image is very important to the emotion, particularly when you're using that image to have the audience identify with it." The truth of that maxim has no better illustration than here, where a threat is implied by the massiveness of the policeman's head. But for all the danger implicit in his appearance, the officer's voice and manner are calm, soft, neutral; he is no bully, and the tension of the scene arises partly out of the contrast between the way he behaves and the way he looks. "There are plenty of motels in this area," he tells Marion. "You should've . . . I mean, just to be safe."

When the policeman asks Marion for her license, Hitchcock cuts to a longer shot, looking across Marion toward the face peering into her window. The effect is eerie: we see a desperate movement of the woman's body as she conceals her purse, digging furtively, while over her shoulder a large head, rather like a masked man, stares down at her. The artificiality of the back projection helps in giving the image a sinister, dreamlike quality; it is a privileged moment in the film, a picture worthy of the surrealists, especially in the way it combines absolute clarity of presentation with the vague aura of a sexual nightmare. There are no gauzy, shadowy, expressionist techniques in what we see, and yet it is deeply evocative, with the power of staying in our minds quite apart from its function in the plot. Indeed this whole episode is memorable for qualities other than the ones that are normally associated with Hitchcock's art. True, he is dealing with the ordinary ingredients of suspense, putting impediments and dangers in Marion's path as she tries to flee with the money; but he generates a relatively mild *degree* of suspense, nothing like the hairbreadth intensity of his true thrillers. The scene is impressive more for the anxiety and strangeness in the imagery, which creates a dream world out of perfectly mundane, daylight ingredients.

After checking Marion's Arizona license plate, the policeman allows her to go on, but it is clear from his dour looks that he has grown suspicious. As Marion drives away, Bernard Herrmann's theme starts up again; Marion glances in her rear-view mirror, and from her point of view we are shown the patrol car following—a black, minatory shape which is all the more striking because there is nothing but a sunlit, empty road before us and behind. Straining, nervous, Marion approaches a roadsign, *Right Lane for Gorman,* and turns off. With a sigh, she watches the policeman disappear along a different fork of the road.

With this relaxation of tension, the theme music fades, and a dissolve takes us to a subjective view from the window of Marion's car as it enters a nondescript town. The traffic has grown heavy, and the back end of an oil truck obscures most of the scenery. After a moment we see Marion slowly driving into a used car lot. Her subsequent encounter with a car dealer in Gorman is a fine blend of comedy and suspense: We laugh at the fast-talking, bow-tied salesman (John Anderson), who mistakenly thinks he has a fickle woman on his hands, and at the same time we share Marion's anxiety when she discovers that the policeman has followed her into town. The setting is still another image of dreary, commercial America: from real-estate offices we have moved to highways, and now to a small strip of concrete decorated with plastic banners and filled with last year's cars. The lot is modest, never ostentatiously satirical, but it helps give the first third of *Psycho* the atmosphere of a wasteland.

As Marion waits for the salesman, she buys a paper, scanning it for news of her crime; while she reads, the highway patrol car drives past, U turns, and parks across the street. Marion declines the salesman's offer of coffee, saying, "No thank you. I'm in a hurry and . . . I just want to make a change." She glances across the way, and Hitchcock gives us another of his carefully designed subjective views: In a longshot, we see the police car and the partolman standing beside it, leaning against the doors with outstretched arms. In the background, in the gap between two buildings, there is a small, wire-fenced vacant lot, an expression of the hopelessness Marion must feel. The salesman walks away to have Marion's car checked in his garage, and she is left fully exposed to the policeman's stare; gripping her handbag tighter, she looks back at him across the road, an occasional car passing between them. When the salesman returns, he finds that Marion has already made her choice. "That's the one I'd have been for myself," he says expansively. "Go ahead, spin it around the block." But Marion is ready to buy. "You *are* in a hurry aren't you," the salesman remarks. "Somebody chasing you?" She won't even question the price, and the salesman quickly drops his friendly banter: "I take it you can prove that car is yours." She asks for a ladies' room and goes inside; from a high angle, we watch her as she takes out her registration papers, never looking at herself in the mirror. She removes the money from its envelope, and in a close-up we see her hands as she counts off seven hundred dollars over a dirty sink (a nice contrast to the spotless facilities at the Bates Motel). Briskly, she repacks her purse and goes out of the washroom. As she and the salesman enter the office to close the deal, we see the patrolman across the road get into his car and drive over to the lot. When Marion comes out, she hurriedly climbs into her new white car, the camera panning to catch her face as she drives off, diverting our attention so that we are frightened when we hear a shout: "Wait!" It is one of the attendants, bringing a suitcase from the car Marion has abandoned. At last she drives away, and the puzzled salesman walks forward, frowning. Just behind him is the patrolman, in a good position to see the license of the departing car.

This last shot has underlined the futility of Marion's situation, and now, as we watch her driving again, her panic gives way to total darkness and confusion. The brief montage of sights and sounds that follows is a perfect evocation of Norman Bates' philosophy: "People never run away from anything. We're all in our private traps." The farther Marion drives, the more oppressed and lost she becomes. The car is like her cell; night gradually falls around her, flashing lights from the highway shine in her eyes, and she imagines the voices of everyone she has left behind. At first the camera is at a slight distance from her face, so that her hands are visible on the wheel. As she nervously bites her lip, Herrmann's theme music begins, and we hear the used car dealer speaking: *"Heck, officer, that was the first time I ever saw the customer high-pressure the salesman."* The policeman responds: *"I better have a look at those papers, Charlie."* Hitchcock dissolves to an absolutely flat, straight road seen from Marion's point of view. The sky above is a dull white, and on either side of the road there are nearly tree-less fields. When we cut back to Marion the image has grown slightly darker. We hear the voice of her boss, talking to the secretary in her office: *"Carolyn, has Marion come in?" "No, Mr. Low-rey, but she's always a bit late on Monday morning."* Each time we return to a view of the road the darkness has grown, until the cars ahead turn on their headlights. *"Call her sister,"* we hear the boss saying. *"I called . . . and she doesn't know where Marion is any more than we do . . . she's as worried as we are."* It has become so dark that now we can see Marion's face only in a small circle of light at the center of the frame. We hear Mr. Lowrey again: *"Wait a minute . . . I remember seeing her driving . . . Carolyn, call Mr. Cassady."* Now the road ahead is completely dark, with only the headlights visible, and when Hitchcock cuts back to Marion's face he has moved the camera in very close, so that she is given barely enough room to move her head. Lowrey is talking to Cassady: *"For heaven's sake, a girl works for you ten years, you trust her!"* Cut back to the road again, and then back to Marion, the camera moved still closer, her face almost lost in the gloom. As she imagines the voice of the oilman Cassady, she smiles wryly: *"Well I ain't about to kiss off forty thousand dollars,"* Cassady says, *"I'll get it back and if any of it's missing I'll replace it with her fine soft flesh."* Bernard Herrmann's theme has now reached a fevered pitch, and we see a couple of drops of rain spatter on Marion's windshield. She

looks up anxiously at the clouds; suddenly the rain breaks loose
very hard. Her wipers come on, silvery streaks ticking back and
forth, lit up by the oncoming cars. When we next see her face the
camera has moved even closer; at one moment she is lost in darkness, but then her entire head is caught by the harsh lights of a
passing auto, and she is forced to close her eyes.

Notice that the power of this sequence is another testimony to
Hitchcock's notions of "pure cinema." Janet Leigh's face is nicely
expressive, but the effect is due less to acting than to the expertise
with which images and sounds have been manipulated. A tremen-
dous anxiety is generated by the gradually accelerated tempi of
music and editing, by the steady movement of the camera in toward
Marion, by the obsessive voices, the growing darkness, the flashing
lights, the sudden deluge, the hypnotic rhythm of the windshield
wipers. All this takes us closer to the realm of pure nightmare, and
prepares us to enter the world of Norman Bates.

Slowly the frenzy begins to lessen. The rain still pours down, but
there are fewer lights on the road. When Hitchcock shows us
Marion again, his camera has moved back a little; she is frowning,
trying to see into the darkness. Far ahead we can make out a single
dim light, barely visible through the rain. As Marion's car moves
closer we see the light emanating from the windows of a low, flat
building, and from a taller structure on a hill behind it. Herrmann's
music ends on a deep minor chord; the only sound is the rain and
the slap of wiper blades. The wipers clear the window, as if a curtain had been parted to begin a whole new arena for the film. We
see a neon sign: *Bates Motel.* Two or three more cuts between
Marion's face and the view ahead, and we are close enough to read
the word *Vacancy.* The car noses in toward a plain wooden building, closer and closer, and then stops.

Hitchcock has said that the horror-movie effects in this phase
of his film—an old dark house, a witch-like woman, stuffed birds,
etc.—are "to some extent, quite accidental." Northern California
is full of houses like the Bates', he tells Truffaut. "I did not set out
to reconstruct an old-fashioned Universal horror-picture atmosphere. I simply wanted to be accurate." But in the very juxtaposition of a rundown motel and a massive Gothic building, a "vertical
block and a horizontal block," as he calls them, he stresses the basic

incongruity which gives *Psycho* much of its unsettling power. Thus, when Marion Crane checks through the empty motel office and goes out on the porch to look up at the house on the hill, we are given a radically new imagery that comes as a shock: We see a decayed Victorian mansion, very like the spooky old San Francisco house that had figured in *Vertigo*. The building is obscured by darkness, but the rain has slackened and two lighted windows at the corner of the upper story are clearly visible. As Marion watches, someone glides past one of these windows—a tall thin old lady, walking slowly, holding herself very erect. In the brightness of the room, her shape is a little blurred and ghostly. Marion blows the horn of her car, the door of the old house bangs open, and Norman Bates comes running down with his umbrella. (Some cheating here, perhaps, since one doubts that he could have changed clothes so rapidly.)

I have already noted the excellence of Hitchcock's casting. Tony Perkins is never effeminate, but his sensitive youthfulness, his gawky posture and the flexibility in his wrists all suggest that he is a mother's favorite. During the fifties he had given a fine performance as a neurotic baseball player in Robert Mulligan's *Fear Strikes Out,* but the intensity and the potential mania in his personality had never been so well employed as here; he may be remembered for the rest of his life as Norman Bates. He is, of course, able to shift from innocence to evil with only the slightest inflection of his features, and when we first meet him, we are disarmed by his boyish deference. "I didn't hear you in all this rain," he apologizes, and motions to the office. "Go ahead in please." The two figures enter, the camera set at eye level, looking straight down the registration desk. A mirror on the far wall catches Marion's reflection and we see both sides of her face; Norman crosses to the other side of the counter, the characters facing each other in exact profile. We can see Marion sigh with relief, and on the folded newspaper sticking out of her purse we read one word of the headline: *Okay.*

The Marion Crane plot, now almost over, has struck many people as an elaborate red herring; but repeated viewings should convince us that *Psycho* has more than shock value. Hitchcock has given his film an extraordinary formal perfection, setting its major characters off against one another, not in a rigid symmetry, but in a way that enriches the story with mysterious contrasts and echoes.

In order to describe this effect, one needs the musical analogy that Hitchcock and many of his critics have suggested: it is as if the film were composed of two contrasting movements which are unified by having certain motifs and themes in common. I have already tried to indicate how Marion's "daylight" America of fast-buck neurosis is balanced against Norman's "night" America of psychotic sexual repression; and yet such descriptions are a bit too schematic. When we watch the film, Marion and Norman somehow *evoke* one another, like characters in a dream. Albert LaValley has beautifully explained this quality as a world where "one experience pulls together threads of many past ones." Other critics have described it as a type of "doubling," an effect one encounters repeatedly in Hitchcock's American films, where the stories are built around mirror-image relationships or subtle parallels between "good" characters and "bad" ones. In *Psycho* he is working once again with these doublings and counterpoints; he even changed the name of one of Robert Bloch's characters from "Mary" Crane to "Marion," so that it would suggest the mirror-image of "Norman."

Norman's half of the film begins just as Marion's is ending, and here, where the two lives overlap, Hitchcock has joined their stories with a number of thematic and visual echoes. As Marion and Norman face each other across the motel desk, they are posed symmetrically. One is female, the other male; one is fair, the other dark. Yet they both have aquiline profiles, wide shoulders, and slender, bird-like bodies. If we do not get the point, Hitchcock reinforces it: After Marion has signed the register with a false name, Norman turns to get a room key, asking her to write down her home address. We cut to a close-up of Marion glancing surreptitiously down at the folded Los Angeles *Times* in her handbag. "Los Angeles," she says. Next we have a close-up of Norman with his back turned. He reaches out for a key to room number three, pauses, glances surreptitiously over his shoulder, and moves his hand down to number one. "Cabin One," he says. "It's closer if you want anything. Right next to the office." Though we do not understand Norman's behavior when we first see the film, it is clear that both characters have something to conceal; the point has been underlined by matching Norman's behavior with Marion's, close-up for close-up.

When she enters Cabin One, Marion is even more relaxed, though she holds her handbag to her bosom with both arms. She can see that Norman is attracted to her, and the smile on her face indicates that she is touched and amused by his bashful puritanism. The camera follows Norman as he goes across to open the windows. "Stuffy in here," he says—another irony that escapes us. The room is neither rich nor new, but it is a clean, well-lighted place. We see the dark frame of a bathroom door, and pictures of birds on the walls. (Later, when Sam and Lila are put in another room of the motel, we discover that bird pictures are exclusive to the first cabin.) Norman smiles shyly and indicates a comfortable-looking bed. "Well," he says, "the mattress is soft, there's hangers in the closet, and stationery in the desk with 'Bates Motel' printed on it, in case you want to make your friends back home feel envious. And the, uh . . ." He turns, switching on a light to the bath. It is so white in there that the camera can barely see; we notice neatly folded towels, a glistening white sink, the edge of a white shower curtain. With this gesture, Norman's identity with the world of motherhood, Sunday school, and spotless plumbing is made complete. "The bathroom," Marion says, speaking the word for him, as if he were an amusing child, "Yes," Norman answers pregnantly. Then he moves forward with a polite and friendly expression and suggests that Marion might like to come up to the house for a bite to eat. "I don't set a fancy table," he says, "but the kitchen's awful homey." Again the two actors are shown facing each other in exact profile, and again Marion's face is reflected in a mirror on the opposite wall. "I'd like to," she says, and Norman leaves, promising to be back with his "trusty umbrella." He is a strange, somewhat troubling young man in a distinctly eerie environment, but his gentleness and his kindly, self-depreciating humor elicit our trust.

This scene, except for a brief close-up of Marion when she says "bathroom," has been photographed in a single take. Now, as Norman leaves, Marion is seen from the doorway, the room behind her in clear focus. She looks down at the key in her hand and sighs rather grimly. Herrmann's music begins playing the same theme we heard when she prepared to leave home, and the camera follows her as she moves about the room, unpacking. More details become visi-

ble—one wall has flowered paper (later we realize that the flowers
help conceal a peephole), and the decor is homey and attractive, in
marked contrast to the dingy, uncurtained hotel where Marion and
Sam were discovered at the beginning of the film. Marion remembers the money; after a brief search for a hiding place, she decides
to fold it up in her newspaper and place it in full view. Just at this
moment she hears distant voices and walks over to the open window, where from her perspective we again see the house on the hill.
The rain has stopped; there is some light in the sky, and several
dark billowy clouds which give the house a classic horror-movie
appearance. The voices come from a lighted upstairs window, where
Norman is arguing with an old woman: "No, I tell you, no!" the
woman says. We make out a few phrases: "By candlelight, I sup-
pose . . . young men with cheap erotic minds." Norman yells, "Shut
up! Shut up!" The downstairs lights come on, and we can see him
returning to the motel.

Marion walks out to the porch to meet him. He comes around
the corner, carrying milk and sandwiches, and the camera swings
around to view the actors in the same pose we have seen before;
for the third time they are shown facing each other in exact profile,
but this time it is Norman's face which is reflected, in a window of
the motel. He is apologetic about his mother ("What's the phrase
. . . she isn't quite herself today."); hesitating to eat in Marion's
bedroom, he proposes the office instead, but the office is "too offi-
cious," so he invites Marion into the "parlor" behind. As he
switches on the light, we see Marion's slightly astonished reaction:
Hitchcock cuts from her face to a shot of a giant stuffed owl, its
wings spread in flight, mounted high up in a corner of the room
where it casts forbidding shadows on the ceiling. Another cut reveals a stuffed raven, its beak creating a dagger-like shadow on the
wall beyond. Now we see Norman leaning over, arranging food on
a table: the room is relatively dark, filled with depressing Victorian
bric-a-brac, and as Norman stands the camera looks up at him from
a low angle, so that the wings of the stuffed owl are spread out
behind him. He gestures to Marion and they sit facing each other,
Norman leaning forward like a good boy in church, with sinister
shadows gathering around him. Marion is clearly put off by the
creepiness of the place, but she seems to feel no particular threat.

She begins to eat, unaware that she is being "stuffed" like the creatures around her. When Norman remarks, "You eat like a bird," she only glances wryly at the walls and remarks, "You would know, of course."

It is worth pausing here to consider Hitchcock's fascination with birds. We do not ordinarily think of them as fearful creatures (*The Birds* will make a great point of that), but in *Psycho* they are associated with all sorts of anxiety and horror. As we have seen, Robert Bloch's novel contains no mention of them, although he does refer to a "stuffed squirrel" in the kitchen at the Bates' house. Even before *Psycho,* however, in the short television film "Banquo's Chair," Hitchcock used a bird motif which had relatively little to do with his plot. "Banquo's Chair" tells the story of a retired detective (John Williams) who organizes a dinner party and arranges the table so that a suspected killer will be facing an open doorway. He hires an actress, an elderly woman disguised as the murder victim, and gives her instructions to appear in the door during the meal. The detective and his accomplices are to pretend that nothing strange is happening, and the killer will be frightened into a confession. When the time comes, everything goes according to plan; but as the confessed killer is being led away, a little old lady arrives to explain that she is the actress and has been delayed. We have already seen that "Banquo's Chair" has some technical features in common with *Psycho;* notice, too, that it uses the figure of an old woman as the instrument of horror. Perhaps most interesting, as Steve Mamber has pointed out (see bibliography), the story is filled with bird references. The detective remarks that he has taken up bird-watching as a hobby: "You'd be surprised how many people are intrigued by it," he says. In planning his trap, he makes sure that the apparition of the "ghost" will be perfectly timed: "We won't bring her on with the soup, that would be rushing it. We'll bring her on with the pheasant." All during dinner, conversation keeps drifting back to the subject of birds; Williams, for example, jokes that he caught a brace of partridge last week, at a market.

As far as I can tell, Hitchcock shows no particular interest in birds before "Banquo's Chair," but in his next two feature films they seem to have taken an extraordinary hold on his imagination. In his interview with Truffaut, he remarks on the significance they had for *Psycho*. "I was quite intrigued with them;" he says, "they were like symbols. Obviously Perkins is interested in taxidermy since he'd filled his mother with sawdust. But the owl, for instance, has another connotation. Owls belong to the night world; they are watchers, and this appeals to Perkin's masochism. He knows birds and he knows that they're watching him all the time. He can see his own guilt reflected in their knowing eyes." As I have previously indicated, *Psycho* is everywhere concerned with "watching." Norman Bates, a bird-like man, watches Marion Crane, who was previously watched by a policeman and who is herself associated with birds. We, as members of the audience, are bird-watchers, implicated in Norman's voyeurism but also passive and knowing witnesses to his crimes. By the end of the film, we will become uncomfortably aware of the identity between our eyes and those of Alfred Hitchcock— we are detached, ironic observers, like the "cruel eyes" that Norman fears in the insane asylum, which have the power of "watching . . . all the time."

Norman explains to Marion that his taxidermy never involves "beasts." "I think only birds look well stuffed," he says, "because they're, well, kind of passive to begin with." In their passive role as watchers, the birds are simply mirrors to guilt. They are like the audience at an ordinary movie, or like the bird-watcher detective and his friends in "Banquo's Chair," who sit around a table, ostensibly chattering away but really staring at a killer, waiting for him to crack. On the other hand, the stuffed owl on Norman's wall is not presented merely as a watcher; he is a predatory beast, posed with his wings extended and his claws outstretched. Norman himself, when he becomes a murderer, is associated with a beak-like knife, and with the shrill, high-pitched shriek of Bernard Herrmann's music, which sounds like the cry of a maddened bird. Hence the passive, repressed act of "watching" in Hitchcock's films nearly always carries with it the capability of acting on what is seen. *The Birds* watch their prey in order to pounce upon it, just as Norman Bates is moved to kill Marion after he has watched her, just as the detective in "Banquo's Chair" watches for the right moment to seize a killer. Significantly, the tension in *Rear Window* results from the fact that the man who watches is imprisoned in a wheel chair, powerless to act directly on his emotions; almost no one in a Hitch-cock movie can remain a neutral observer.

If the watching birds in *Psycho* are symbols, they will not submit to an easy decoding. Like Melville's whale or Virginia Woolf's lighthouse, they are obsessive, dreamlike objects, highly ambiguous because they are capable of functioning in so many different yet subtly related roles. They can be passive or active, murderous beasts or observers of other people's guilt; they are sometimes victims and sometimes victimizers. In the scene between Norman and Marion in the parlor of the Bates motel, we sense their ambiguity every-where—not only in the presence of the stuffed creatures themselves, but in the mannerisms of the actors and in their dialog. For exam-ple, at a particularly intense moment in Norman's conversation about his mother, Hitchcock cuts to a close, low-angle profile which is filled with menace: Behind Norman, the owl in the upper corner of the room seems to be swooping down, aimed directly at his head. As Robin Wood has observed, Norman "becomes, simultaneously, the bird (from his relation to it) and its victim (from his position under it)." There are few movies, few works of any kind, that can evoke such complex responses out of a single composition.

But the impressive scene in the parlor is once again generated out of very simple means. Most of the time, Hitchcock simply cuts back and forth between his two characters, showing them from nearly identical angles, his camera positioned a bit low and far enough back so that we can see their postures and the sinister am-biance of the room. We find ourselves sharing Marion's uneasiness, as well as her sympathy toward Norman. He is hungry to talk with someone, and though he is resigned, he seems well-adjusted enough to be ironic about his problems: "A boy's best friend is his mother," he says, looking glumly up toward the old house, then smiling quickly. He appears to have sacrificed his life out of compassion for a woman he claims is mentally ill; now and then, of course, his sad-ness and irony give way, revealing his true madness. He talks about insane asylums with the glazed eyes and the angry, intense voice of a man who has been there, and he is chilling about the death of his mother's former lover. "It's nothing to talk about while you're eat-ing," he says with a smile. Throughout, the imagery and the conversation are laden with hints of Norman's insanity, little jokes about what he has done to Mom: Marion looks at the stuffed birds and comments, "A man should have a hobby." Norman replies sweetly, "Oh, it's more than a hobby" (a line spoken by Bela Lugosi in Louis Friedlander's *The Raven,* a rather bad thirties horror film that features a stuffed bird exactly like the one in Norman's parlor). At one point in talking about his mother, Norman leans back in his chair and abstractedly strokes one of the pieces of taxidermy; on the walls behind him we can see, in addition to the giant owl, a series of pseudo-classical paintings which feature naked women in vaguely erotic poses. "A son is a poor substitute for a lover," he says. "Who'd look after her . . . she'd be alone up there. It would be cold and damp like a grave."

But in spite of our growing uneasiness, Norman throws us off guard, partly because of his kindness toward Marion. He can sense that she too has a problem, and he seems to be telling her about his life partly in order to unburden her. His philosophy, however, is hardly designed to offer consolation. When Marion evasively remarks that she is running away to a "private island," he becomes dreamy and abstract: "People never run away from anything," he says, "We're all in our private traps, clamped in them, and none of us can ever get out. We scratch and claw, but only at the air, only at each other." Marion cannot grasp the full significance of this statement, which is actually Norman's one moment of painful lucidity; nevertheless, she can understand how it applies to her own circumstances. "Sometimes," she says, "we deliberately step into those traps." After a brief silence, Norman softly replies, "I was born in mine." When she asks him why he does not go away, Norman only smiles ruefully: "To a private island, like yours?"

This momentary glimpse into a life more troubled than her own helps Marion decide to return to Phoenix. If her life has been a "trap," it is at least better than Norman's, better than the circumstances she placed herself in by stealing the money. "We all go a little mad sometimes," Norman tells her, "Haven't you?" "Yes," she says, "just one time can be enough." She still has the power to undo her crime, and at the end of the scene she thanks Norman because he has helped her more than he realizes. She is going back to Phoenix, she says, because "I stepped into a private trap back there, and

I'd like to go back and pull myself out of it." Before she goes, she tells Norman that her real name is Crane.

But when Marion returns to her room, Norman's boyish manner falls away and our point of view is radically changed; the intense moment in the parlor, where for the first time we encounter an actor whose presence dominates the screen more than Janet Leigh's, has served to make a major transition. Until now, we have seen events largely as Marion sees them. Here, for a single scene, we take Norman's point of view, in preparation for the even greater disorientation that will result from the shower murder. We see Norman standing in the door of the parlor, looking after Marion as she goes; a brief subjective shot gives us a glimpse of her back as she walks out the door. Norman's face is in darkness, and the giant shadow of a raven on the wall behind him seems at first to be a sinister bird perched on his shoulder. He walks forward a pace, into the light of the office, and pops a candy into his mouth to nibble. As he checks the register and the false name Marion has written there his expression is cool, slightly amused. Now he goes back into the parlor, closing the door. In close-up, his shadowed face moves across the room, past the birds and the erotic pictures: He stands at the wall next to Cabin One and listens, his eyes cast sideways. As he turns toward the wall, Hitchcock cuts to a view over his shoulder; he is looking at a painting which depicts two rather devilish looking men in the act of raping a plump, nude woman. Norman removes the painting to reveal a large ugly hole which has been ripped in the wall behind it; just beyond, in the wall to Cabin One, there is a second, very tiny hole emanating a shiny point of light—the first in a series of circles and holes, feminine symbols that will recur like repetitions in the formal scheme of a poem.

As Norman leans forward to look we are given a subjective view through the jagged edges of the peephole. Marion stands near the open bathroom door, taking off her clothes. She is again shown in her bra and half slip, and there are a couple of bird pictures on the wall behind her. We cannot help but admire her body as she casts aside the dress; when her hands go up to remove the slip, the males in the audience watch expectantly, sharing in Norman's secret desires. But just at the moment when we are about to witness the nude Janet Leigh, Hitchcock cuts to an extreme close-up of the side of

Norman's eye. He is peering with an unblinking intensity through the small bright hole, and the effect is slightly vertiginous: On the one hand, some of the audience are as interested in the half-naked woman as he is—they have happily looked at her twice before, and now they itch with expectation that she may finally cast aside the brassiere. On the other hand, the spectators have been forced into a certain detachment, becoming watchers twice removed. We sit in the dark room of the theatre, voyeurs ourselves, watching the bright image of a voyeur's eye; at the same time, the man on the screen, unaware of our presence, stands in his own dark room, his pupils focusing on a shaft of light. Thus Hitchcock does more than manipulate our response; he creates another "doubling" effect, this time between the audience (especially the male audience) and the actor. He teases us, inviting us to become aware of our relation to the photographic image.

When next we see Marion through the little peephole, she is putting on her bathrobe. For just a moment, we glimpse what looks like an exposed breast, and then she turns and walks out of view. Norman's head withdraws, a little circle of light sliding down his cheek. He replaces the picture, and in a slightly longer view we see him turning away, an angry look on his face. With a swift little jerk of the head, he looks up at Mother's house, thinks a moment, and then walks deliberately out: the camera watches him go up the hill, walk into the house, pause at the foot of a big stairway, and then saunter morosely off toward the kitchen, where he sits thoughtfully at a table.

We now cut to Marion, who is seen in virtually the same pose at a writing desk; she is examining her bank account, trying to compute how she will repay the seven hundred dollars she spent on her car. Grimly she tears up the notes she has taken, and walks into the bathroom. A close-up of the toilet seat shows her flushing away the bits of paper.

What follows may be the most horrifying *coup de theatre* ever filmed. If we approach the film innocently, we become victims of an outrageous joke, a trick that is in such bad taste we feel guilty for having appreciated it. We are left without bearings, because the whole order of expectations which we carry to the ordinary narrative, the whole basis of our engagement, is suddenly extirpated.

Of course we have sensed the threat implied by the sinister atmosphere of Norman's parlor, the danger latent in that spooky house which supposedly contains a madwoman. Perhaps we have even guessed that Marion will be killed. Certainly an audience which had grown accustomed to Hitchcock's television series was prepared for the unexpected, and in any case the advertisements for *Psycho* carried a warning that patrons would not be seated after the film began. They knew that *something* was going to happen, and they had developed a taste for slightly sick humor. But they could not have expected the suddenness, the absurdity, the apparent finality of what actually occurs.

One might think that repeated viewings would make the shower murder lose its force. Certainly when Janet Leigh is no longer remembered as a "star" the scene will have lost some of the impact it had for contemporary audiences. In fact, however, repeated exposure only deprives us of the "surprise" effect. We are so shaken that every subsequent viewing fills us with an uneasy anticipation, a *malaise* that begins from the moment Janet Leigh steps into the shower. "Surprise" gives way to Hitchcock's other favorite effect, "suspense," which he defines as "providing the audience with information that the characters do not have." When I myself first saw the close-up of Marion closing the bathroom door and her naked back as she removes her robe, I anticipated mainly the erotic pleasure of watching her body (though the care with which all this is rendered made it clear that something was afoot). In all my later viewings, erotic emotions are mingled with discomfort: How soft, how incredibly vulnerable she now is; how squeamish one becomes at the thought of a knife. We see a close-up of her legs as she drops the robe and steps into the tub, drawing the curtain; with mounting uneasiness, we note how defenseless she is in that position, how insecure the footing must be in there. The details of each successive shot make the audience think about the danger in waiting: her long throat raised to catch the shower spray; her fragile arms; the antiseptic, surgical whiteness of the bathroom tiles. Finally, when her killer enters the room, the montage ceases momentarily. We are allowed to see the menace before she does, in a single long take with both figures shown in the frame at the same time. From a high angle, almost at the level of the shower spigot, we watch Marion's face at the lower part of the screen; behind her there is an expanse of translucent shower curtain. Through the spray and the curtain, we can see the bathroom door opening. The camera slowly moves down past Marion's shoulder, with only the sound of water falling, as a tall, blurred shape approaches, standing just outside the shower. Suddenly the figure whips open the curtain; we hear an extraordinary shriek of music, and cut to the silhouetted head of an old woman, only the eyes visible, a giant knife in her upraised hand. A close-up shows Marion turning, water in her face; a still closer view shows her mouth opening; a third, very extreme close-up shows the mouth screaming, droplets of water falling from the lips—a vaginal counterpart to the phallic knife.

It is of course an extremely violent scene, but we are actually shown very little. What we have in fact is a perfect illustration of the psychological power of montage, the illusion of violence and sex created entirely out of what Hitchcock has described as "putting . . . little bits of film together." As V. F. Perkins has observed, the use of montage here works to "aestheticize" the horror. By choosing not to show the scene in a single take, Hitchcock maximizes the psychological impact while at the same time preventing our being overcome by an alienating nausea. Out of more than fifty separate shots, only one shows a knife entering a body: in a close-up of a bare abdomen, we see an artificial-looking image of a knife blade moving slowly in to make a tiny puncture. Even in this explicit shot, there is no blood. Most of the sequence is made up of simple cross-cutting between a dark, maniacal figure lifting an arm to strike and Janet Leigh's face backed up against the tiles, her head bobbing from side to side as she screams. There are several overhead views, using a stand-in for Leigh, which were shot in slow motion, the actress placing her arms so as to mask her breasts from movie censors. (As usual, the guardians of morality were more upset by the possibility of nudity than by excessive violence—they were, in effect, linking themselves to Norman Bates.) Three times we are shown blood mingling with water at the bottom of the tub (Hitchcock once told a little boy that he used "chocolate sauce"), but we are never shown any wounds. In fact, Janet Leigh's body seems as unmarked at the end of the sequence as it was at the beginning; even the bathroom stays relatively white, most of the blood running neatly down the drain.

Hitchcock has said that it took him seven days to film the sequence (perhaps slyly comparing himself to God), and in an interview in the first issue of *Take One* (1966) he remarks that there were "seventy-eight cuts for forty-five seconds of film. That meant you got pieces of film no bigger than two or three frames." Later, in his interview with Truffaut, he says that there were "seventy camera set-ups." Presumably he meant to say "cuts"; in any case, his memory does not seem to be exact. In the print I have examined, where the sound track is unbroken, there are between fifty-five and sixty-five cuts, depending on where you start counting, and the stabbing alone, not including the long final shot or anything before the ripping aside of the curtain, runs for nearly fifty seconds. The average number of frames per shot is around fifteen; the briefest shot runs for eight frames, and the longest for thirty-five. Yet Hitchcock's description is true to the spirit of the sequence I have studied; with dozens of brief shots, all of them as carefully worked out as a ballet, he created the impression of sustained, frenzied violence. And the same effect, one feels, could not have been obtained by more "realistic" methods, where the camera would be set back at a distance to observe the whole action in a single take. In fact he had previously experimented with shooting a violent struggle in a single shot. He tells Truffaut that for the fight between Raymond Burr and James Stewart in *Rear Window,* "I had filmed the whole thing realistically. It was a weak scene; it wasn't impressive. So I did a close-up of Stewart's face and another of his legs; then I intercut all of this in proper rhythm and the final effect was just right."

The "proper rhythm" is of course important, but so far as I can tell, the creation of this rhythm, whether in a poem or a novel or a film, is not simply a matter of quantity. Generally speaking, the shots at the opening and closing of the shower sequence remain on the screen longer than the ones in the middle, but rhythm is also created by other factors—by the alternation between closer and longer views, by the movement of the actors, and ultimately by Bernard Herrmann's music. In fact, the sequence is all the more impressive for the way it orchestrates nonmusical sounds. As I have said, Hitchcock originally planned to have no music at all for the murder scenes; at the beginning what we hear is intensified by the echoes from the tiled walls. A toilet flushes; a curtain opens and closes; paper is torn off a bar of soap; a steady downpour begins. For about thirty-five seconds we hear only the water, and then as the killer rips open the curtain, Herrmann's music begins—an extremely high-pitched string passage, punctuated by Marion's screams and a series of notes that are like whistles. When the stabbing is over and the old woman is seen dashing out of the room, the music abruptly shifts into a loud but slow sequence of bass chords in a minor key, and we watch Marion's face as she slides down the wall, her eyes staring, her outstretched hand reaching slowly to grasp the shower curtain. The music stops and she falls forward, her head striking the floor outside the tub with a dead flop; during the camera's long final shot there is almost a complete stillness, only the sound of running water and the gurgle of a drain.

It is a paradox (perhaps the most important paradox of the many that we can find in Hitchcock's work) that the power and vividness of the shower murder should depend on the formal, highly orderly way it is designed. It is as if orderliness and anxiety were interdependent, each feeding the other. A remarkable number of the shots have been planned so as to create an easily recognizable visual pattern: for example, there is an eleven-frame subjective view showing a corner of the ceiling through a torrent of water; in a quite geometrical arrangement, we see a curtain rod, some moulding at the edges of the ceiling, and an uplifted hand with a knife blade. The whole sequence was elaborately thought out, in fact, sketched out in advance by Hitchcock. Thus we begin with a very close view of Norman Bates' eye as he peers through a hole, and we end with a close view of a hole (the bathtub drain), dissolving into an extreme close-up of Marion Crane's dead eye. (The circular design in these shots is repeated by another close-up, aimed directly into the round shower spigot as it sends out water.) In addition to the symmetry of these compositions, we also have a neat balance between the montage of the stabbing and the slow, complicated tracking shot which closes the sequence. After showing us a stream of blood running down the drain, Hitchcock dissolves to Marion's eye; it is an extraordinary image, as beautiful as it is unremitting.

The camera moves slowly back, and we see a single drop of water on her cheek, like a tear. Her mouth is open, her lips pressed against the tile floor, her face dead.

The power of the shot derives chiefly from the fact that we are looking at a still photograph. To achieve the absolute stasis of death, Hitchcock directed his technicians to rephotograph sections of a single frame; in what must have been a very difficult process, successive pictures were taken, each at a slightly greater distance from the frame, so that the camera appears to pull slowly back from Marion's eye, tilting slowly to echo the spiral of water down the drain. Hitchcock cuts away briefly to the running shower spigot in order to mask the return to the original moving picture image. When he cuts back to the face, his camera begins a slow pan to the right, past the toilet, rising, pointing out through the open door toward Marion's bed. Then it moves slowly forward, the sound of running water growing dimmer in the background as we close in on a night table and the folded newspaper where Marion has concealed her stolen money. The camera pauses, stares, and moves to the right again, up the flowered wallpaper and over toward the open window. Outside we can see the eerie silhouette of the Bates' house, and in the distance we hear Norman's voice shouting "Mother! Oh God, Mother! Blood!"

The neatness of this final camera movement, its sheer elegance, tends to remind the audience of the director's presence. It is a chilling authorial flourish, as if Hitchcock could not resist taking a bow (or acknowledging responsibility for what he had achieved). From this point, he needs to do very little in order to disturb his audience or raise gooseflesh. The simple fact of what has happened, and its conjunction with everything that has gone before, is enough to leave us shattered, unable to continue watching *Psycho* as if it were an ordinary movie. Hitchcock has not only teased us with our voyeurism, he has punished us. It should make the male audience even more uncomfortable to reflect that even while they watched the stabbing, so carefully designed to suggest both a mother's revenge and a kind of rape, they were hoping to catch a glimpse of a naked body.

The remainder of the story works to "discover" and unmask Norman Bates. In fact, if we discount the long opening development of Marion Crane's character, the film has the same "three times is a charm" structure as Robert Bloch's novel. First Marion encounters Norman; her death brings Arbogast; his death brings Sam and Lila. With each encounter the boyish surface of Norman's personality fades a bit more and we penetrate deeper into his house, until his secret is disclosed. But the murder of Marion Crane has generated such anxiety in the audience that the suspense mechanics of the plot can do their job without much further help from Hitchcock, who felt that the protagonists of the second half of the film were basically unimportant. As he told Peter Bogdanovitch, "The audience goes through the paroxysms in the [rest of] the film without consciousness of Vera Miles or John Gavin. They're just characters that *lead* the audience through the final part of the picture. I wasn't interested in them." For this reason, we can treat the second half of *Psycho* in a somewhat less detailed fashion, concentrating on Hitchcock's real interests, a series of brilliant images which elaborate the themes he had already introduced.

Consider, for example, Norman's attempts to conceal what "Mother" has done. The sequence was influenced partly by a television film Hitchcock had made three years earlier called "One More Mile to Go," which begins with a brutal, drawn-out killing, and then shows the murderer (David Wayne) methodically packing the body into the trunk of his car. Subsequently, when Wayne tries to drive off and dispose of the body, he is stopped on the roadside by a policeman, in a scene rather like Marion Crane's encounter with the highway patrol officer. But in almost every way *Psycho* is a superior reworking of these ideas. After Norman dashes into Cabin One, we are given a vivid series of close-ups: his back frozen in the doorway of the bathroom; his face as he grips his mouth in shock and nausea and spins back against a wall; one of the bird pictures falling to the floor and striking his foot. In succeeding images, we are shown every bit of the determined and apparently dutiful way he cleans up—as Leo Braudy has said, Hitchcock shows us "the most characterless place on the American landscape . . . become characterless again." Braudy is wrong, however, when he suggests that we identify with Norman because "Our hands hold the mop and swirl the towel around the floor." Actually, there are no subjective shots in the sequence; from now to the end of the picture we remain somewhat "outside" of Norman, and Hitchcock will not use the subjective camera again until Arbogast and Lila Crane explore the Bates' mansion. We see terribly vivid, starkly photographed close-ups of Norman washing blood off his hands, neatly scrubbing stains off the basin; we see his mop cleaning out the tub, his arms wiping the tiles—but none of this is shown from his point of view. If we feel somehow implicated in Norman's desire to smother the crime, it is because, even in the midst of our horror, we are relieved to see the gore disposed of, the immaculate bathroom restored. The sequence is beautifully counterpointed with the violent montage that preceded it, and it is wonderfully satirical, revealing how a sanitary exterior can repress chaos. At the same time, it communicates Hitchcock's own passion for order. He has not been afraid to show his face, as well as ours, in the satirist's mirror.

Raymond Durgnat describes the effect of this satire when he says that Hitchcock convicts us all of a "lingering nostalgia for evil." As a further example of what Durgnat means, notice how we grasp or laugh painfully when Norman tosses the Los Angeles *Times* into the trunk of Marion's car, sending it down into the muck with everything else—our motives, perhaps, are less pure than his. Also, when the car momentarily stops sinking into the swamp, we feel a very complex and ignoble emotion: We have to laugh at Norman's embarrassment, the neatly wrapped-up evidence stuck on the surface of a pond; but at the same time we hold our breath, hoping it will sink. Such moments, incidentally, are not unique to *Psycho*—they are worked into Hitchcock's most glossy and conventional films, like *Dial M for Murder,* where we find ourselves hoping that Ray Milland will discover his watch has stopped so that he can call home in time to have his wife murdered. Are we mad when we laugh at tricks like these, as Durgnat suggests, or are we merely human?

After Marion's car has gone down, we are left with Norman, who stands beside the swamp (a nice contrast to that shiny bathroom), nibbling candy like a strange bird, smiling with satisfaction. The image dissolves, taking us to the Loomis hardware store and to a new "movement" of the film. It is Saturday, December nineteenth, and Sam Loomis is writing a letter to Marion: "Dearest right-as-always Marion: I'm sitting in this tiny back room which isn't big enough for both of us, and suddenly it *looks* big enough for both of us." It is another sick joke, a joke that is compounded when the camera pulls back from Sam, tracking down the aisle of the store. Loomis Hardware is not just depressing; it looks like a torture chamber. The walls are covered with knives; a scythe hangs from the ceiling; boxes of weed killer line the shelves. A little old lady is talking to a clerk about insecticides; she is holding a can of "Spot Insect Killer," reading the instructions, hoping that the poison won't cause the little fellows too much pain. Once again murder and mayhem are being contrasted with small town niceness, as if the grotesque horrors were related to the bland surface.

First the anguished Lila (Vera Miles) enters this scene, and as she talks with Sam we see a face looking in the window of the store. It is the detective Arbogast (Martin Balsam), and the two close-ups which introduce him are reminiscent of the highway policeman who looked into the window of Marion's car. Again the head is massive, expressionless, staring, and again it is shown against a whitened, artificial-looking background which gives the image a dreamlike quality. Both figures of the law are depicted as "watchers," peering in at other people's lives; but the menace expressed in the first pictures of Arbogast is only temporary—in contrast to the highway cop, he is a short ununiformed fellow, who turns out to be more kindly than we expect. We follow him as he searches for Marion in hotels and rooming houses all around Fairvale, and when he finally encounters Norman Bates sitting on the porch of the motel, nibbling candy and reading a magazine, he becomes virtually our agent, the instrument of our curiosity if not our identification.

Arbogast drives up to the Bates Motel around dusk, and Norman invites him into the office, switching on the lights. Hitchcock avoids the symmetrical two-shot he had used earlier for the meeting between Marion and Norman; instead, the scene is developed by a series of gradually larger close-ups, the camera sometimes at a slightly low angle, sometimes at a high angle, emphasizing conflict and anxiety. Arbogast is not especially intimidating, but he is clever, and we laugh at Norman's discomfort even while we pity him a little. The episode is beautifully acted; Perkins is especially effective when he is forced to acknowledge that he remembers the runaway secretary ("You know how you make a mental picturization of something."), or when he leans over the motel registry, looking at the name that the detective is pointing out: In a giant close-up, we see the underside of his chin, the bird-like working of his jaws and neck, the little bobble as he swallows candy. Throughout the interview, his eyes glint in the growing darkness—he is nervous but also a bit mean. In the last shot, he is shown leaning against the outside of the motel, smiling with a certain evil satisfaction as the detective drives away. Unlike Marion, he seems to feel no guilt for his crime, only an anxiety to keep it concealed.

Later, returning to the motel during the night, Arbogast makes a series of discoveries. Through his eyes we see the stuffed birds in Norman's parlor; through his eyes we look up at the old house on the hill. When he foolishly walks into the Bates home, we are shown his view of the hallway, the kitchen, the long stairway to Mother's room. A brief close-up shows his feet going up the steps, and then the camera is aimed at his face, rising with him as he mounts the stairs.

In the interview with Truffaut, Hitchcock provides an interesting account of how this scene came to be photographed in a single take:

> One day during shooting I came down with a temperature, and since I couldn't come to the studio, I told the cameraman and my assistant that they could use Saul Bass's drawings. [Bass, who was interested in the picture, had been allowed to sketch out some ideas for this sequence.] Only the part showing him going up the stairs, before the killing. There was a shot of his hand on the rail, and of feet seen in profile, going up through the bars of the balustrade. When I looked at the rushes of the scene, I found it was no good, and that was an interesting revelation for me, because as the sequence was cut, it wasn't an innocent person but a sinister man who was going up those stairs. Those cuts would have been perfectly all right if they were showing a killer, but they were in conflict with the whole spirit of the scene.

For instructive comparison, note the moment in *Frenzy* when Richard Blaney ascends a darkened stairway to commit murder: Hitchcock offers a montage of the killer's feet, his hands on the rail, his determined face, his murder weapon. In *Psycho* the point was to emphasize the innocence, vulnerability, and complacency of a victim. Thus Hitchcock avoids cutting until Arbogast has nearly reached the top of the stair. We see a door opening, and then a cut to a dizzying, high-angle shot: "Mother" comes bounding out of her room, accompanied by Herrmann's frantic, shrieking music, meeting Arbogast at the head of the stair, slashing his face with a knife. Notice that the high angle does more than obscure Mother's face; it gives us the feeling that we are looking down into an abyss, thus creating a moment which is highly typical of Hitchcock's films. He has repeatedly shown his characters dangling or falling from high places, but these acrophobic scenes are not simply the mechanics of suspense; they are poetic figures, perfect expressions for the chaos which disrupts the lives of his protagonists. As we have seen, Hitchcock admits that his own anxieties are held in check by a compulsive neatness; his greatest fear, expressed in virtually every film he has made, is the loss of equilibrium. Here, the surprise and shock which explode upon Arbogast are mirrored in the dreamy image of him falling backward down the stair, his arms flailing for balance, his eyes wide with fear and confusion. When he strikes bottom, we see the old woman rush on top of him; the camera shows her upraised arm, and as the knife plunges down, the screen fades to darkness.

Time passes, and Sam and Lila, who have remained behind, grow worried. As they prepare to investigate on their own, the imagery portends still further disasters: Sam decides to visit the motel, and Lila waits in the darkness of the hardware store, light from a room behind her making a halo at the edge of her blond hair, a display of rakes forming a circle of hard spiky points around her head. But Sam discovers nothing (Norman is out by the swamp again), so he and Lila go together to visit the local sheriff and his wife (John McIntire and Laureen Tuttle). Truffaut has criticized the scene with the sheriff as a "letdown," and Hitchcock himself seems to agree with Truffaut's judgment, saying that he finds the characters "dull"; nevertheless they are in some ways typical of his work, and there is an important justification for them. Sheriff and Mrs. Chambers are shown in their home, surrounded by domestic sweetness; later, we see them coming out of an archetypal church (called simply "Fairvale Church"), and the sheriff's nice, motherly wife tells Sam and Lila to forget about Norman Bates: "It's Sunday," she says, "come to our house for dinner." The irony of these details should be transparent if we have sensed the relationship between Norman Bates' provincial gentility and his psychotic lusts. In the quaint but repressive atmosphere of Fairvale on a Sunday morning, it is almost as if evil did not exist—but of course we know that it does. Hitchcock has repeatedly set his American films in attractive little communities like this one, full of decency and Sunday-go-to-meeting pleasantries. Again and again he has created satire by showing evil intruding on the small town ethos—one thinks of *Shadow of a Doubt,* and especially of *The Trouble with Harry,* where a group of lovable characters keep dragging a body around the sunlit, autumnal landscape of a New England village. A related theme can be detected in *North by Northwest,* which uses the midwestern prairies and the bourgeois solidity of the presidential monuments at Mount Rushmore as scenes of terror. Bodega Bay in *The Birds* is perhaps the ultimate representation of these destroyed Edens, and in the center of that film we have another small town American family. It is as if the evil were fostered by the complacent setting, even if on the surface the two things do not always seem causally related.

We can see Hitchcock's satire at work in the way he juxtaposes the sheriff and his wife with a brief scene involving Norman Bates. The sheriff tells Sam and Lila that Norman's mother has been dead for ten years; as a matter of fact, his wife helped choose the dress Mrs. Bates was buried in ("periwinkle blue," she says sweetly). Meanwhile, back at the old house, Norman is shown putting "Mother" in the fruit cellar. In one of the most vertiginous and disturbing images of the film, the camera follows him up the stairs, rising beyond him into an inky blackness, executing a 180 degree turn, tilting downwards as it does, so that it surveys the stairwell from a great height. As Norman carries the limp body downstairs, we hear a cackling voice which sounds like a comic parody of a little old lady: "No! I will not hide in the fruit cellar! Hah! You think I'm fruity, huh?" Norman is highly deferential, but Mrs. Bates puts up no struggle at all; in fact, the camera angle makes her look like an invalid. The scene is a brilliant expression of sickness and evil, and Hitchcock follows it with a derisive comment:

Norman descends the stair, the screen fading to darkness, then brightening to show us the following day. It is Sunday, and the camera is aimed at the white spire of the Fairvale church.

The pretty Sunday makes a wonderfully incongruous setting for the unveiling of Norman's secret. When Sam and Lila arrive at the motel, the old house is bathed in sunlight, looking prosaic at last. In the motel office, Hitchcock repeats the compositions he had used earlier for the confrontation between Marion and Norman. He poses the characters symmetrically, on either side of the registration desk, and once again he achieves a "doubling" effect: Lila of course resembles her sister Marion, but for the first time we realize that there is an odd physical resemblance between Sam and Norman. Both are tall, with dark hair and eyes, their profiles set off against one another. Sam, however, is not birdlike; in fact he reminds us of a strapping, "healthy" version of Norman. In the subsequent arguments between these two, and especially in the scenes where they struggle with each other, the movie seems to be verging on psychomachia, as if Norman's potential consciousness, his possible daylight existence, were forcing itself upon him.

But of course Norman cannot stand this sort of exposure. Ultimately he forsakes his identity completely, becoming little more than a double for his mother's corpse. After we have seen the film several times, Lila's explorations of the Bates mansion begin to look like a sort of violation. At first we have the titillation of discovery and suspense, but later we are aware of Norman's anguish; Hitchcock cuts back and forth between Sam's relentless questioning and Lila's investigations, until the madman begins to look like a trapped insect. Nevertheless, the camera in these sequences gives most of its sympathy to Lila, becoming her eyes as she climbs the hill and watches the old house drawing nearer and nearer. The subjective tracking, intercut with closer and closer views of Lila's face, is almost a trademark of Hitchcock's style, important chiefly for the way it lends an otherworldly atmosphere to his films. Lila seems to be gliding, not walking toward the house—an eerie effect which is perfectly appropriate to our fearful anticipation of what she will discover. If we have not yet guessed the secret of that house, it seems alive with menace; if we have, it becomes a symbol of Norman's mind.

Hitchcock has crammed Mrs. Bates' bedroom with Victoriana, even though the nineteenth-century trappings are distinctly anachronistic. According to the sheriff, Mrs. Bates has been dead for only ten years, but her house and her possessions belong to a different age. Nearly all the details Hitchcock shows us are designed to express Mrs. Bates' repressive character; a meticulously ordered washbasin; a rack of flowered dresses which button at the neck; a bronze moulding of a pair of hands, quite delicate and beautiful, but with lace cuffs down to the wrists. The most prominent object in the room is a massive bed, neatly made, with an extraordinarily deep outline of a body in its center—a sign not only of how long Mrs. Bates has lain there, but of the way her body has impressed itself on Norman's consciousness.

Norman's own room is even stranger: It retains the atmosphere of a nursery, with antique toys and a painting of a sailing ship. The bed is tiny, and atop the rumpled spread there sits a cuddly bunny rabbit, no doubt one of Norman's first stuffed animals. Amid all this juvenalia, Lila discovers vestiges of the adult Norman: a phonograph with a recording of Beethoven's "Eroica" (A curious detail— is it supposed to suggest "erotica"?), and a neatly bound, untitled book, embossed in gold. Hitchcock leaves the contents of this book a mystery, showing us only the beginnings of a reaction on Lila's face as she opens it to read; in Robert Bloch's novel, however, we learn that the book is full of pornographic pictures.

Meanwhile Sam, whose life is governed by his need for money, is in the motel office grilling Norman, accusing him of killing Marion in order to get the forty thousand dollars. If the audience has not yet guessed Norman's secret, they hope he will break loose and get to the house before Lila discovers Mrs. Bates. Of course he does just what the innocent spectators want, bashing Sam on the head and rushing toward the house, and the climactic moments of the film are structured with the "rising curve of interest" that Hitchcock has said he likes to give all his pictures. In rapid succession, he piles suspense upon shock upon shock. Retreating from Norman, Lila moves down to the fruit cellar. The audience is frantic with expectation, especially when Lila sees Mrs. Bates sitting beneath a naked light bulb, her back turned away. The first shock comes when Lila wheels Mrs. Bates around, discovering a skull where the face should be. She screams, knocking the light bulb into a crazy, looping spin. The second shock arrives when Norman prances in, announced by Herrmann's music, dressed like Mother, grinning madly and wielding a knife.

Sam, who is just behind, restrains Norman, and the ensuing struggle is posed rigidly, like a piece of statuary. Sam grasps Norman by the wrist, and with his other arm he takes a strangle hold; but the pain on Norman's face is completely out of proportion to his physical suffering. His eyes squint and his mouth contorts wildly. His back arches and his fingers claw at the air as he sinks to the floor, his dress ripping apart and his wig falling off. He seems to disintegrate before our eyes, in the tradition of old-fashioned monster movies like *The Mummy;* in fact, the sequence ends with a close-up of the decayed face of Mrs. Bates, lying on the cellar floor.

After this climactic frenzy, the audience is allowed to relax for several minutes while the "meaning" of Norman's behavior is explained in the light of psychiatry. The scene changes to the Fairvale courthouse. It is evening (the date should be December 20th, but the calendar on the wall says December 17th); Sam and Lila, together with the sheriff, a few officials, and a psychiatrist (Simon Oakland), have gathered to sort out what has happened. Hitchcock says that this rather long sequence was photographed in a single day, and his lack of interest is reflected in the banality of it all. The best critics of *Psycho* have argued that the scene is ironic, but in my own mind there remains some doubt whether Hitchcock intended it that way. His work has been damaged more than once by attempts to introduce straightforward psychoanalysis; for example, in *Spellbound* (1945) and later in *Marnie* (1964) he tried to tell Freudian detective stories, with somewhat mixed results. Both films offered elaborate explanations for abnormal behavior, and both films, despite their effective moments, degenerated into a silly, middlebrow rationalism. As Albert LaValley has observed, "There is a desire on Hitchcock's part to link up with orthodox Freudianism as the system that most closely approximates his vision of the unconscious, but the films never quite connect." I cannot agree with LaValley's notion that Freudianism has "little to do with the major intensities" of Hitchcock's films—indeed it seems to me that the whole emotional effect of his work, from its humor to its terror, can be most accurately explained in orthodox Freudian terms. Still, Hitchcock is not in the business of making Freudian allegories, and there is no question that the psychiatric explanations in *Psycho* are flat, dull, and pompously acted. Hitchcock's "problem" is not so much that Freudianism doesn't fit, but that his imagination is far richer and more persuasive than ordinary analytical reasoning. Paradoxically, the explanations at the end of *Psycho* come to his aid, because they do not successfully reduce Norman to a case history. In fact, they raise as many questions as they answer.

We are given a few simple details about Norman's past life. We learn, for example, that he murdered his mother and her lover, and that he killed at least two women before Marion. We are told that Mrs. Bates was a "clinging, demanding woman," and that her "dominant personality" has at last won the battle for Norman's self—but most of this we have probably guessed by now. The psychiatrist does not try to explain Norman's sexual frustrations, and the extraordinary fusion of revenge and rape in the shower murder is allowed to speak for itself. Moreover, when we come to the question of Norman's guilt, we are not offered an easy way out. As the psychiatrist explains it, the "Mother" side of Norman's personality does not necessarily correspond with the real Mrs. Bates. Norman was obsessively jealous of his mother, and so he naturally assumed that she was jealous of him. As a result, he created a version of Mrs. Bates, a figure who would seek violent revenge whenever "she" felt Norman was aroused by another woman. He sought to make his mother share in his crimes; he had murdered her lover, so she was made to murder his.

As I say, this explanation is badly played; the analyst is patronising and pomaded, strutting around the little office like a lawyer in a courtroom. But when we think about what he says, we find it far from simple-minded. He emphasizes neither personal guilt nor determinism. He asserts evil and injustice, but he makes us blame Norman as much as his mother. Of course, the film does not stop here, and in the final images, as powerful as anything in Hitchcock's work, we are left confronting the mystery in all its explicitness. A policeman takes Norman a blanket; off screen we hear an old woman's voice saying "Thank you," and when the policeman leaves we see Norman sitting in a completely bare, white-walled room. At first the camera is at a considerable distance, with Norman at the left of the frame, his bony figure wrapped in the blanket. To the right is the corner of a barred window, and between these two dark shapes there is nothing but empty, weatherless space. The camera tracks slowly in toward Norman's face, and as music begins to play, in a soft, poignant strain, we listen to the voice of Mrs. Bates. As Ernest Callenbach has observed, it is probably the most striking and appropriate use of internal monologue in all cinema. "It's sad," the voice says, "when a mother has to speak the words that will condemn her own son."

To what extent is this the voice of the real Mrs. Bates, speaking to us from the grave, and to what extent is it only Norman's imaginary version of his mother? Are we looking at a man who thinks he is his mother, or at a mother who has taken possession of her son? "I couldn't allow them to believe I would commit murder," the voice says. The figure on the screen, which is now so ambiguous that it cannot be given a name, shakes its head sadly, its eyes concentrated into tiny dark points. "They'll put him away now, as I should have long ago." (We remember Norman's reluctance to have Mother committed.) "He was always *bad*," the voice says (we remember that Norman once tried to blame everything on Mother). "As if I could do anything," it says, "except sit here and stare, like one of his stuffed birds." (We imagine what guilt Norman must have felt when he looked at Mother's empty eye sockets.) As a final strategy, the mad voice claims that it will show "them" that it can't even move, can't even swat a fly. The face glances down at a fly on its wrist, and then the eyes glance up. It is a powerful, frightening, yet somehow witty moment, a perfect finish, and we find ourselves smiling along with the face on the screen: for the first time in the film, a pair of eyes are looking not at an indeterminate imaginary space, but at *us*. (A moment rather like the confrontation in *Rear Window,* where we spy on a killer through James Stewart's telephoto camera lens, and then discover that he is staring directly back.) Once again we are reminded of our role as watchers, and those sinister eyes meet ours almost like an act of defiance. We remember Norman's comments on insane asylums—"institutions," with "cruel eyes studying you." The image of that grinning, malevolent face is intended to make us uncomfortable in more ways than one.

As Herrmann's theme music plays, we see Mother's skull gradually, ever so slightly superimposed over Norman's face; then a lap dissolve shows Marion's white car being dragged out of a muddy swamp. In its economy and its formal perfection this last image is highly satisfying, but it teases us, leaving us in doubt. Marion Crane's murderer has been uncovered and made to pay, but who or what was that murderer? We are offered very little besides the formal pleasure of a neat ending—Hitchcock even avoids using the potential lovers, Sam and Lila, to give his film an optimistic romance. In subtle ways he reminds us that we all suffer, on the lower frequencies, from Norman Bates' conflict with civilization. We laugh uneasily, aware that *Psycho* has been a monstrous joke, and a joke partly on us. Some viewers have been offended by the humor; but if we could not laugh, if we could not appreciate the grisly wit, we would all go mad.

summary critique

In November 1960, a nineteen-year-old boy from Milwaukee stabbed a girl to death. He entered a plea of not guilty by reason of insanity; just before the stabbing, his lawyers explained, he had seen *Psycho*.

I bring up this grotesque incident not because I think *Psycho* is a public danger (although perhaps in a certain circumstance it might be), nor because I have an explanation for what happened in Milwaukee. I only want to point out how unsatisfactory is one of the major critical theses about Hitchcock's work: To Robin Wood, who has written beautifully about *Psycho,* Hitchcock's movies have a "therapeutic" value; both the characters and the audience, Wood says, become "cured of some weakness or obsession by indulging it or living through the consequences." This, it seems to me, is altogether too safe and rational an explanation for why we appreciate Hitchcock. He is not a rationalist, and he resists complacency in any form, even the form that would suggest that we can somehow be cured through art. It may be, as I have previously suggested, that Hitchcock's subject matter allows him to indulge his *own* dark instincts and obsessions, and it may be that a film like *Psycho* works upon some members of the audience in a similar fashion. Nevertheless the case for the "therapeutic" value of any art has yet to be proved, and the stabbing in Milwaukee presents a crucial test for the hypothesis.

Should we then go to a nearly opposite extreme and regard *Psycho* as a rebellion against civilization, a sick, antihumanist work masquerading as an entertainment? Something like this view is suggested by Raymond Durgnat, who takes Hitchcock as a sort of nihilist in sheep's clothing. Durgnat clearly admires *Psycho,* and in my view he provides a more useful way of talking about the film. Nevertheless, his arguments about Hitchcock strike me as unsatisfactory. I quote them here at length, because they contain stimulating insights:

> Hitchcock's films constantly tend towards a disillusionment which, far from being liberating, is paralyzing. Hitch as baddie—the sardonic mastermind suggested, yet camouflaged, by the title master of suspense—seems matched by a fearfulness which has prevented Hitch from expressing his personal vision other than coyly, or in the fates of subsidiary characters, or in the "religious absurdity" of Hitchcock the poet. Hitchcock described to Truffaut his vision of a film about food and what happens to it (as waste, it's flushed into the sea). The vision hardly needs psychoanalysis. Aldous Huxley, I think, first used of Swift that phrase "the excremental vision," which happily describes a certain kind of pessimism (Sade, Huxley himself, Celene, the swamp-and-bathroom syndrome in *Psycho*). It's probably truer to say that Hitchcock's best films leave a nasty taste—so long as the phrase is used admiringly, as it might be of the novels of Gerald Kersh. Kersh is, perhaps, the man Hitchcock ought to be, to be truly Hitchcock—only Hitchcock, quite reasonably, prefers to use his insights in order to tease, to play, to be an affable bogeyman (*The Strange Case of Alfred Hitchcock,* III).

Brilliant as many of these remarks are, there is something decidedly wrong in saying that Hitchcock "ought to be" Gerald Kersh. In the first place, Hitchcock is a far superior artist to Kersh (How many people, even among the intelligentsia, have read one of Kersh's unexceptional novels?); in the second place, Hitchcock is not in active rebellion against life, à la Sade and Swift, and his "coy" mannerisms are as much a part of a "personal vision" as his nastiness. Certain aspects of the bourgeois stability Hitchcock satirizes are valuable to him, both in his life and in his work; he needs stability in order to maintain what Durgnat elsewhere calls a "carefully limited existence." We admire his films because they are both disturbing *and* pleasurable, the pleasure often deriving from his playful attitude toward his materials, as if he were only just contemplating taking off a mask. Moreover, some of his characterizations—the Janet Leigh and Tony Perkins roles in *Psycho,* the James Stewart role in *Vertigo* and *The Man Who Knew Too Much*—indicate that he can be compassionate even while he is being satiric. It is true that Hitchcock is a pessimist, and that psychoanalysis would reveal his "excremental vision" (the same could be said of every good satirist), but Durgnat is wrong to imply that the "Hitchcock touch" is the result of hypocrisy or a lack of self-examination. The formal perfections in Hitchcock's films, together with his sly humor, are elements in a studied pose, a serene and rather detached attitude toward life that lets the audience—most of them—enjoy their nightmares.

Hitchcock is neither a therapist nor a cowardly monster; he is primarily a craftsman in the best sense, a formalist who has raised the thriller genre to its highest levels, often transcending it. His major themes, as I have already indicated, can be found in every suspense story, and particularly in his sources—in John Buchan, in Daphne DuMaurier, in Patricia Highsmith, even in Robert Bloch. Naturally Hitchcock's choice of the suspense mode over all the others can be taken as an indication of a temperament, an attitude toward experience; again and again he has chosen to make us feel the precarious balance between order and chaos, between innocence and evil, between repressions and anxiety. In the later half of his career, when his technical skills were at their peak, he gave these themes their most intense expression, making more profound and troubled pictures. *Psycho* is one of the masterpieces of the late period, but it cannot be reduced to a thesis about insanity or to a nihilistic vision. It has a fascinating structure which may tempt the critic to look for an underlying argument: A motherless female character is played off against a male character whose mother is too much with him. City is played off against country, money against sex, realism against expressionism. The whole texture of the film is loaded with jokes, symbolic details, and self-conscious manipulations of psychoanalysis. But *Psycho* is not making a statement; it is, to use another of Durgnat's well-chosen phrases, a "battery of emotional provocations." The neat juxtaposition of Marion Crane and Norman Bates is not created for the sake of an allegory, but for its teasing emotional effects, its range of moral possibilities.

Psycho is hardly a "coy" film, but for all satire and gore, it helped to make Hitchcock a very rich man. It was nominated for five Academy Awards (winning none): Janet Leigh, Hitchcock, John Russell, art directors Joseph Hurley and Robert Clatworthy, and set decorator George Milo. It had an immediate influence on commercial filmmakers (William Castle's *Homicidal,* Robert Aldrich's *Whatever Happened to Baby Jane*), as well as upon the "art" movie (Polanski's *Repulsion*). It virtually established a whole subgenre of psychotic thrillers, including such obvious derivations as the English *Psychomania* and the Italian comedy *Psycosissimo,* and it was at least indirectly an impetus for the new wave of bloody horror movies that are still with us. It thus became not only a classic film but a minor social phenomenon. I have neither the space nor the ability to analyze that phenomenon here, but I will note that the contemporary reviewers did not appreciate Hitchcock's artistry, much less recognize that he was well into a major phase of his career (see Bibliography). The passing of time has vindicated critics of various nationalities who championed *Psycho* when Hitchcock was still regarded as a "mere" entertainer. In France, there was Jean Douchet and the writers for *Cahiers du Cinema;* in England, Robin Wood and Ian Cameron; in the United States, Andrew Sarris and, somewhat later, Peter Bogdanovitch. Some of their views are summarized in the Bibliography, and I hope my indebtedness to them has been clear throughout this study. If anything, *Psycho* looks better today than in 1960, when Hitchcock's popularity as a TV personality and his great success at the box office tended to make intellectuals leery. As I have indicated throughout this discussion, repeated viewings of the film increase one's respect for the subtlety of it all, for the sheer manipulative logic of the conception and for the beauty and simplicity of the visual design. But manners have changed since 1960; perhaps we now have a greater appreciation of dark humor, and we certainly have a clearer historical perspective on *Psycho.* Whatever the reason, Hitchcock's picture now seems both profound and artful.

Psycho is especially important to us retrospectively, because we can see that it stands at an interesting juncture in the development of the American popular film. It is midway between the repressive manners of the classic Hollywood studio movie (Janet Leigh wears a bra) and the "liberated" ethos of the R-rated contemporary film (Janet Leigh is shown in bed with a man at midday). It might seem to point toward the "new" morality, but it belongs, as Durgnat has pointed out, squarely within the traditions of the "old" morality. It gives the audience satisfaction by titillating their libidos, but it makes them uneasy accomplices to a psychopath, cautious about their instincts. Clearly it does not induce us to live the sexually repressed life of a Norman Bates, but neither does it make us think that sex is good and innocent.

In much the same way, *Psycho* stands midway between the conventional Hollywood narrative and the self-conscious style of the art film. It concentrates on plot, not on character or philosophy; but, like *Rear Window,* Hitchcock's other exercise in "pure" cinema, it will not allow us to enjoy our fantasies in complete security. It plays jokes with us, and it slyly comments on the making and watching of movies. It belongs to a relatively advanced stage in film history, a period when the artist has begun to contemplate both himself and the "meaning" of a genre such as the horror picture. During the late fifties and early sixties, Hitchcock's ideas about montage had come full circle; he had reached the height of his powers as a teller of conventional stories, and his films began to take on a particularly reminiscent and reflective cast. With the American version of *The Man Who Knew Too Much* and with *North by Northwest* (essentially a remake of *The Thirty-Nine Steps*), he was elaborating and improving his early masterpieces. But in *Vertigo* he tossed the suspense story aside in order to create an extraordinary film about the relationship between obsessive sexual fantasy and reality; and in *Rear Window* and *Psycho* he was using the suspense formula not in and for itself, but partly in order to reveal his whole understanding of the medium. It is no accident, no peculiar foreign affectation, that Hitchcock's face should have appeared in Godard's films, or that Hitchcock himself should have been a shadowy figure who stands in a corridor during Resnais' *Last Year at Marienbad,* or that Truffaut and Rohmer and Chabrol should all have written books about him. Without being aware of it, he had prefigured the European film renaissance of the nineteen-sixties. At first glance, a film like *Psycho* may not seem to have much in common with *Blow-Up* or *Persona;* but look again. Consider its preoccupation with *dopplegangers* and cinematic voyeurism, its overt declarations of the director's presence, its intimidations of the audience.

This is not meant to suggest that Hitchcock is an *avant-garde* intellectual, though certainly he is far more conscious of his art than the public usually realizes. He conceived *Psycho* as an entertainment, like all his other films; but at the same time he regarded it as having certain esoteric values. As he told Truffaut, *"Psycho, more than any of my other pictures, is a film that belongs to filmmakers, to you and me."* For that very reason, he has always been reluctant to talk about the "moral" of the picture. When Peter Bogdanovitch asked him if any moral implications were intended, Hitchcock simply replied, "You can't apply morality to insane persons." Yet clearly the audience of *Psycho*—myself included—tries to attach itself sympathetically to certain of the characters, or to form the sort of opinions one has about the people in any story. Depending on how sophisticated we think we are, we try to feel superior to Sam Loomis when he complains about money; we try to feel wiser than Marion Crane when she insists on "respectability"; we try to pity Norman Bates. But the film will not allow us to settle into these comfortable positions. It is a wonderfully impersonal movie, not in the sense that the author is a cold aesthete, but in the sense that it never gives us a chance to feel secure. Even to the very end, where we think we have Norman Bates perfectly analyzed, we are prevented from measuring out easy judgments, prevented from being sure of ourselves.

Of course impersonality in this sense has often been taken for an Art-for-Art's-Sake aesthetic or for meaningless relativism—consider some of the attacks on literary formalists like Flaubert or Joyce. It is certainly true that impersonality in art can develop its own complacency by simply avoiding the responsibility of judgment; in *Psycho,* however, this is not the case. Norman Bates and his mother are condemned for their acts, and clearly the face that stares at us in the final image is the face of madness and death. Yet even when our sense of justice is satisfied, some of us continue to want Hitchcock to step out from his mask and behave "seriously." Hitchcock himself has said, "If I were telling the same story seriously, I'd tell a case history and never treat it in terms of mystery and suspense. It would simply be what the psychiatrist relates at the end" (interview with Bogdanovitch). Such a remark does not mean that *Psycho* is a trivial work; on the contrary, it shows us very distinctly how the film has overcome the problems of somber, "realistic" movies and novels, which make us too secure with the world of facts. As Geoffery Hartman has written, this sense of security is a "serious contemporary exigency of realism. When empathy becomes conventional and the new or alien loses its aureole of sacred danger, it is increasingly difficult to admit transcendent personality or real difference. . . . It is the familiar world that must now be saved—from familiarity" (*Beyond Formalism*). Partly because of its impersonality and its wit, *Psycho* is able to overcome the familiarity of the thriller and the horror movie, as well as the more pervasive familiarity of realistic case histories. In this sense, it might be said to "save" us.

All this brings us to the paradox of Hitchcock's personality. He is both an entertainer and an artist, a satirist who is well-liked. He lives an orderly and therefore "repressed" life, but he makes films about the breakdowns of orderly worlds. There is a sense in which he, like his characters, is an "ordinary bourgeois," but he is far more sensitive than most, more conscious of absurdities and dangers. Indeed it is this paradoxical quality in his nature that gives his films so much of their power—it is troubling to realize that a sophisticated and diabolic imagination is concealed behind that round, gentle face. One might almost say that Hitchcock's greatness lies in his ability to evoke equally disturbing contrasts within the familiar context of popular entertainments. Even when we forget the plots and the supposed "morals" of his films, certain images haunt us: a dowager putting her cigarette out in the yolk of a fried egg; a country gentleman holding up a missing little finger; a Madison Avenue executive standing on an empty roadway in the midst of a prairie. All these images depend on the stories surrounding them, just as they depend, in a more general sense, upon the format of the conventional suspense story. But they also stand apart, like indexes to Hitchcock's mind. *Psycho* is a great film partly because it has so many of them: the giant stuffed owl over Norman Bates' head; the shower murder; the grinning face of a madman superimposed with his mother's skull. Hitchcock's visual imagination, combined with his understanding of ordinary human fears, helps to make his film a part of the consciousness of anyone who has seen it. *Psycho* affects people across the boundaries of class and even of language; it is, for all its barren and depressing atmosphere, a nearly universal movie.

a Hitchcock filmography
bibliography
rental sources

a Hitchcock filmography

More elaborate filmographies, which list players and technicians, can be found in LaValley's *Focus on Hitchcock,* Truffaut's *Hitchcock*, and Wood's *Hitchcock's Films*.

FEATURE FILMS

1922   *Number 13* (unfinished), *Always Tell Your Wife* (Co-directed by Seymour Hicks).

1925   *The Pleasure Garden*

1926   *The Mountain Eagle, The Lodger*

1927   *Downhill, Easy Virtue, The Ring*

1928   *The Farmer's Wife, Champagne*

1929   *Harmony Heaven, The Manxman, Blackmail*

1930   *Elstree Calling, Juno and the Paycock, Murder*

1931   *The Skin Game*

1932   *Rich and Strange* (in US, *East of Shanghai*), *Number Seventeen*

1933   *Waltzes from Vienna* (in US, *Strauss' Great Waltz*)

1934   *The Man Who Knew Too Much*

1935   *The Thirty-Nine Steps*

1936   *The Secret Agent, Sabotage*

1937   *Young and Innocent*

1938   *The Lady Vanishes*

1939   *Jamaica Inn*

1940   *Rebecca, Foreign Correspondent*

1941   *Mr. & Mrs. Smith, Suspicion*

1942   *Saboteur*

1943   *Shadow of a Doubt, Lifeboat*

1944   *Bon Voyage, Adventure Malgache*

1945   *Spellbound*

1946   *Notorious*

1947   *The Paradine Case*

1948   *Rope*

1949   *Under Capricorn*
1951   *Stage Fright, Strangers on a Train*
1952   *I Confess*
1954   *Dial M for Murder, Rear Window*
1955   *To Catch a Thief, The Man Who Knew Too Much*
1956   *The Trouble with Harry*
1957   *The Wrong Man*
1958   *Vertigo*
1959   *North by Northwest*
1960   *Psycho*
1963   *The Birds*
1964   *Marnie*
1966   *Torn Curtain*
1969   *Topaz*
1972   *Frenzy*

HITCHCOCK-DIRECTED TELEVISION FILMS

More details can be found in Steve Mamber's "The Television Films of Alfred Hitchcock," *Cinema* (Fall 1971); and in Jack Edmund Nolan's "Hitchcock's TV Films," *Film Fan Monthly* (June 1968). Nolan's filmography is reprinted in *Focus on Hitchcock.*

1955   "Breakdown," "Revenge," "The Case of Mr. Pelham."
1956   "Back for Christmas," "Wet Saturday," "Mr. Blanchard's Secret."
1957   "One More Mile to Go," "Four O'Clock," "The Perfect Crime."
1958   "Lamb to the Slaughter," "Dip in the Pool," "Poison."
1959   "Banquo's Chair," "Arthur," "The Crystal Trench."
1960   "Incident at a Corner," "Mrs. Bixby and the Colonel's Coat."
1961   "The Horseplayer," "Bang! You're Dead."
1962   "I Saw the Whole Thing."

selected bibliography

I have included some of the best-known criticism written before 1960, but mainly I have kept to items that are directly relevant to *Psycho*. A more extensive bibliography can be found in LaValley's *Focus on Hitchcock*.

REVIEWS: A SAMPLING OF MAJOR SOURCES, MAINLY AMERICAN

CALLENBACH, ERNEST. *"Psycho." Film Quarterly* (Fall 1960): 47–49. One of the more intelligent of the reviews, though it relegates *Psycho* to the supposedly inferior class of popular entertainment. "*Psycho* is surely the sickest film ever made. It is also one of the most technically exciting films of recent years . . . more imaginative and far more elegantly contrived than the all-out seriousness of *Nun's Story,* not to mention the gigantism of *Ben Hur.*"

CROWTHER, BOSLEY. *"Psycho." New York Times* (June 18, 1960). Crowther likes the film, but calls it relatively slow-paced and heavy-handed. He chose it as one of the ten best pictures of 1960.

DYER, PETER JOHN. *"Psycho." Sight and Sound* (Autumn 1960): 195. A favorable review, which concludes by saying, "Of course, it is a very minor work."

HATCH, ROBERT. "Films." *The Nation* (July 2, 1960). Hatch is "offended and disgusted." He calls Hitchcock a "pander of vicarious perversion," and says that "The clinical details of psychopathology are not material for trivial entertainment."

MCCARTEN, JOHN. "Current Cinema." *The New Yorker* (June 25, 1960): 70. Describes the film as "rather heavy-handed . . . a dawdling Alfred Hitchcock apparently uncertain just what to do with a young lady who has pinched forty thousand dollars."

Newsweek. (June 27, 1960): 92. "Sporadic chills," mainly in the first half of the picture.

Time. (June 27, 1960): 51. "Director Hitchcock bears down too heavily . . . stomach-churning horror."

BOOKS

AMENGUAL, BARTHELEMY, AND BORDE, RAYMOND. *Alfred Hitchcock.* Premier Plan, No. 7. Lyon: Serdoc, 1960. A very brief survey.

DOUCHET, JEAN. *Alfred Hitchcock.* Paris: Editions de l'Herne, 1967. Concentrates on the later films, with emphasis on the relationship between suspense, metaphysics, and psychoanalysis.

LAVALLEY, ALBERT J., ed. *Focus on Hitchcock.* Englewood Cliffs, N.J.: Prentice-Hall, 1972. A valuable anthology of criticism with a fine introduction and bibliography.

MANZ, HANS PETER. *Alfred Hitchcock.* Zurich: Sansouci Verlag, 1962. Mainly German translations from *Cahiers du Cinema.*

PERRY, GEORGE. *The Films of Alfred Hitchcock.* London: Studio Vista Ltd., 1970. A rapid survey of the films. Some interesting stills.

ROHMER, ERIC, AND CHABROL, CLAUDE. *Hitchcock.* Paris: Editions Universitaires, 1957. The first book on Hitchcock. A controversial. attempt to see him as a Roman Catholic artist.

WOOD, ROBIN. *Hitchcock's Films.* London: The Tantivy Press, in association with A. Zwemmer Ltd., 1965. An excellent book, and the only serious one in English (excepting Durgnat's book-length series of articles for *Films and Filming*). Tries to repair the excesses of French criticism while defending Hitchcock against Anglo-American snobs. Concentrates on the late films, interpreting them in highly moral, Leavisite terms.

INTERVIEWS

BOGDANOVITCH, PETER. *The Cinema of Alfred Hitchcock.* New York: The Museum of Modern Art, 1962.

CAMERON, IAN, AND PERKINS, V. F. "Interview with Alfred Hitchcock." *Movie,* No. 6 (January 1963). Reprinted in Andrew Sarris' *Interviews with Film Directors.* Indianapolis: Bobbs-Merrill, 1967.

GUNN, JOYCE W. "Hitchcock et la TV." *Cahiers du Cinema,* No. 62 (Aug.–Sept. 1956): 6–7.

TRUFFAUT, FRANCOIS. *Hitchcock.* New York: Simon and Schuster, 1967. This book of interviews may not be as definitive as its publishers claim, but it is nevertheless an important source of information. Interesting for the occasional sparring matches between directors.

ARTICLES

BRAUDY, LEO. "Hitchcock, Truffaut, and the Irresponsible Audience." *Film Quarterly* 21, No. 4 (1968): 21–27. One of many attacks on the Truffaut interview book. Makes Hitchcock sound like a moralist anyway, but contains brilliant insights, emphasizing voyeurism and audience manipulation. Reprinted in *Focus on Hitchcock.*

Cahiers du Cinema, No. 39 (October 1954); No. 62 (August–September, 1956). Hitchcock issues. Pre-*Psycho,* but containing important general essays by Bazin, Chabrol, Astruc, and Truffaut.

Cahiers du Cinema in English, No. 2 (1966). Reprints some of the Hitchcock essays from the French editions.

DOUCHET, JEAN. "Hitch et son public." *Cahiers du Cinema,* No. 113 (October 1960): 7–15. One of the earliest serious treatments of *Psycho.* Discusses the suspense techniques of the film in relation to *Rear Window.* See also Douchet's *Alfred Hitchcock.*

DURGNAT, RAYMOND. "Inside Norman Bates." *Films and Feelings.* Boston: MIT Press, 1967. Reprinted in *Focus on Hitchcock.* Full of inaccuracies about what happens in *Psycho,* but one of the finest essays we have on the film.

————. "Michael Powell." In *Movie Reader,* ed. by Ian Cameron. Praeger, 1972, 84–87. This article makes Powell's film *Peeping Tom* (1959) sound very like *Psycho,* although it was released slightly earlier.

————. "The Strange Case of Alfred Hitchcock." *Films and Filming* 16, No. 6 (March 1970), through 17, No. 2 (November 1970). An ambitious, brilliant, though often negative series of articles on Hitchcock's career. An excerpt is reprinted in *Focus on Hitchcock.*

FARBER, MANNY. "Clutter." *Negative Space*. New York: Praeger, 1971, 208–11. Farber loves the opening sequences of *Psycho,* hates the rest because he thinks it clichéd.

HIGHAM, CHARLES. "Hitchcock's World." *Film Quarterly* 16, No. 2 (Winter 1962): 3–16. Anti-Hitchcock.

HUSTON, PENELOPE. "The Figure in the Carpet." *Sight and Sound* 32, No. 4 (Autumn 1963): 159–64. A general assessment of Hitchcock, arguing that he is not a major figure.

MAMBER, STEVE. "The Television Films of Alfred Hitchcock." *Cinema* 7, No. 1 (Fall 1971): 2–7.

MAZZOCCO, ROBERT. "It's Only a Movie." *New York Review of Books* (February 26, 1970): 27–31. Uses *Topaz* and Truffaut's interviews to attack overly serious attitudes toward Hitchcock.

MILLAR, GAVIN. "Hitchcock *versus* Truffaut." *Sight and Sound* (Spring 1969): 82–87. Another attack on Truffaut.

PECHTER, WILLIAM S. "The Director Vanishes." *Moviegoer,* No. 2 (Summer–Autumn 1964). Revised version in *Twenty-Four Times a Second*. New York: Harper & Row, 1971: 175–94. Underrates some of the American films, but gives an interesting analysis of the artist.

PERKINS, V. F. "The World and Its Image." In *Film as Film*. Middlesex, England: Penguin Books, 1972: 71–115. In the context of a fine introduction to film aesthetics, Perkins offers as extended analysis of the *Psycho* shower-bath montage.

SARRIS, ANDREW. "Alfred Hitchcock." *The American Cinema*. New York: E. P. Dutton, 1968: 57–61. Short but pithy. Sarris is probably the most influential and embattled critic in America. In my opinion he is also the best. He has had much to do with elevating Hitchcock's later films into major status.

SONBERT, WARREN. "Alfred Hitchcock: Master of Morality." *Film Culture,* No. 41 (Summer 1966): 35–38. Interesting essay on Hitchcock's relationship with his audience.

WOOD, ROBIN. "Psychoanalyse de *Psycho*." *Cahiers du Cinema,* No. 113 (November 1960): 1–7. Early version of the *Psycho* chapter in *Hitchcock's Films*.

rental sources

Cine-Craft Co.
709 S.W. Akeny
Portland, Oregon 97205

Clem Williams Films
2240 Nobelstown Road
Pittsburgh, Pennsylvania 15205

Roa's Films
1696 North Astor Street
Milwaukee, Wisconsin 53202

Twyman Films, Inc.
329 Salem Avenue
Dayton, Ohio 45401

United Films
1425 South Main
Tulsa, Oklahoma 74119

United Films
2903 Louisiana
Houston, Texas 77006

Universal 16
Atlanta, Georgia: 205 Walton Street, N.W., 30303
Chicago, Illinois: 425 North Michigan Avenue, 60611
Los Angeles, California: 2001 South Vermont Avenue, 90007
New York, New York: 630 9th Avenue, 10036